stephenie meyer

queen of twilight

stephenie meyer

queen of twilight

THE BIOGRAPHY

Chas Newkey-Burden

JOHN BLAKE

Published by John Blake Publishing Ltd,
3 Bramber Court, 2 Bramber Road,
London W14 9PB, England

www.johnblakepublishing.co.uk

First published in paperback in 2010

ISBN: 978 1 84454 936 8

British Library Cataloguing-in-Publication Data:

A catalogue record for this book is available from the British Library.

Design by www.envydesign.co.uk

Printed in Great Britain by CPI Bookmarque, Croydon, CR0 4TD

3 5 7 9 10 8 6 4 2

Papers used by John Blake Publishing are natural, recyclable products made
from wood grown in sustainable forests. The manufacturing processes
conform to the environmental regulations of the country of origin.

Internal photographs courtesy of Getty Images, Rex Features and WENN.

For Tal – always beyond beseder.

acknowledgements

With grateful thanks to John Blake, Amy McCulloch, Andy Armitage, Chris Morris, Lucy Bows, Tal Hevroni, Jonathan Sacerdoti and Noga Avital Tairy for their help and enthusiasm.

contents

preface

'We all dream a lot, some are lucky some are not.'
– From the musical *Joseph & The Amazing Technicolor Dreamcoat*

Stephenie Meyer had never thought of herself as a person who encountered a lot of good luck. 'I don't usually have any,' sighed the author. 'I've never won anything in my life, and no one ever catches a fish when I'm in the boat.' So she had no idea, as she closed her eyes and sank into sleep on that night in 2003, that what was going to occur during her slumber would change her life for ever, making her globally famous and enormously wealthy.

It was the first night of June and the summer was well under way. As she slept peacefully, Stephenie sailed into the most vivid dream. In it, she saw an ordinary teenage girl and a young man who was 'fantastically beautiful' – but who was also a vampire. The pair were lying together in an idyllic, deserted meadow in the middle of woodland. Their desire for each other in these tranquil surroundings was visceral and strong, yet all they did was talk. They expressed their yearning for each other and discussed the fact that the vampire was having to restrain himself from attacking her and drinking her blood.

The girl told him, 'I would rather die than stay away from you.'

The vampire vowed in return that he would never hurt her, however much he desired her very lifeblood. The colours and sounds of the dream were vivid; the way the couple discussed their quandary was moving and strangely haunting. The uncommon, potent combination of their innocent love and his sinister urges made this no ordinary dream. It was memorable and overpowering in its forcefulness.

When Stephenie woke from her sleep, she decided this was too powerful a dream just to forget and move on from. So she lay in bed for a while, silently replaying the drama in her head. Then she got up, and as soon as she could she sat down at her desk, fired up her computer and typed in the full details of her vivid nighttime fantasy. But at this stage she was not aiming for fame, nor even publication. She was writing the story with just one reader in mind – herself. 'I had a very specific audience and it was a twenty-nine-year-old mother-of-three,' she said.

She couldn't know it at the time but Stephenie Meyer's story would be read by tens of millions of devoted fans. Her life would never be the same again.

introduction

Stephenie Meyer is a publishing sensation. More than 85 million copies of the *Twilight* series of books sold around the world in the first three years they were on sale – and they keep flying off the shelves. Her popularity is all-encompassing: at several points in 2009 all five of her novels were in the Top 10 of the British and American book charts. The previous year alone she had sold 27 million books in 37 countries. They continue to sell in huge numbers in shops around the world, in the 38 languages in which they have been published to date. Her stories are a cinematic sensation, too. The first film, *Twilight*, alone grossed nearly £200 million worldwide and nearly 10 million DVDs of it have been snapped up by hungry fans. As the sequels to *Twilight* also hit the big screen, there is just as much excitement: when the trailer for the *New*

Moon film was posted online it received a record-breaking 10.6 million page views in just seven days. In the UK alone, it grossed £1 million in advance bookings before it was even released.

As a result of all this comes an even more pertinent figure: Stephenie's personal fortune as a result of her success is estimated to be in excess of £50 million.

At the centre of this whirlwind of hysteria, vampire devotion and financial success sits an unlikely figure. Stephenie is an unassuming, loving mother who is terrified of scary books and movies. She follows the strict guidelines laid down by the controversial Mormon religion. Far from being confident of the commercial potential of her story, she was nearly physically sick with shock when she learned she had secured a book deal. Once the resulting novel, *Twilight*, became a hit she would often vomit through nerves before the public appearances she gave to promote it. She is in some ways an uncomfortable star.

In time, Stephenie's sales could reach the heights of *Harry Potter* author JK Rowling, whose personal fortune as a result of her success is estimated at around £560 million. She is quick to modestly dismiss the very idea. 'We can compare a lake to an ocean: they are both filled with water, but they are not the same thing,' said Stephenie who often pushes aside comparisons between her and Rowling. 'I am a fan of her books. Even if mine are sold in a phenomenal way, there will not be another JK Rowling. Of course, I am flattered when it is mentioned, but that's it.'

Her humble feelings are not shared by many observers. In summing up the appeal of the *Twilight* series, the influential American newspaper *USA Today* cheered, 'Move over, Harry Potter.'

A leading figure in the American book trade agrees: 'Her fans are so loyal,' says book buyer Faith Hochhalter, 'aside from JK Rowling, I've never seen anything on this scale – it's almost rock-star status.'

Loyal indeed: as one 13-year-old fan put it, 'She can make anything interesting. I would read math textbooks if Stephenie Meyer wrote them.'

Make no mistake, young readers are the most critical and volatile of the lot. To build a devoted and loyal fanbase in that age group is no mean feat. The girls who make up the majority of Stephenie's readership pride themselves on their critical faculties. If she was not aware of this already, it was spelled out clearly to her when she was approached by a fan while doing a signing in Salt Lake City. 'You're like my favourite author ever,' said the eleven-year-old. 'I'm a person who judges authors a lot, and I don't have anything bad to say about you. I mean, I'm really tough: I didn't even like Harry Potter!' Another fan in the same city told Stephenie that her novels had stopped her from committing suicide.

Stephenie's influence on her fans is huge. She has even spawned a pop band in tribute to her work – the

Bella Cullen Project, a *Twilight*-influenced three-piece from Texas.

The band members – in common with the majority of *Twilight* fans – are teenage girls. The gender issue is relevant for Stephenie. In writing about vampires, werewolves and aliens in her various novels, she has trodden on some very geeky, and therefore largely *male*, terrain. The paradoxes of her identity are interesting: she calls herself 'a girlie girl' but displays many of the traditional traits of the tomboy. Gender issues aside, though, there can be no doubting her popularity.

So what is behind the appeal of Stephenie's stories? The author herself is none the wiser. 'I don't know,' she said. 'I read a lot of books and some of them that I love are really popular, and there are just others that I just think, "Why isn't everybody in the world reading this book? It's so amazing." Why does it ever happen? I don't know why people respond to these books the way they do.'

But respond they do – in their millions. Stephenie Meyer has struck a chord across the globe and the excitement shows no sign of abating. There is a waiting list of a thousand for the library copy of *New Moon* at one American school.

Not only has she delighted readers, she has also inspired would-be authors. 'Sometimes I feel a little bit like an ambassador for people who want to write because I represent how lucky you can get,' she says. 'For most people it's a really difficult journey – being published, writing your first book, getting out there. For me it's been like a lightning strike, where I went from being a stay-at-home mom to all of a sudden, without much effort on my part, being a stay-at-home mom who has a really great career writing. I like to tell people that it can happen.' She says she merely got lucky, but all of her success is richly deserved. All the same, though, she is correct that her success is a fine example to those who dream of being the next Stephenie Meyer.

Here is her fascinating and inspiring story.

chapter one
a mormon childhood

Twilight is obviously not an autobiographical novel. The author did not spend her teenage years surrounded by vampires and werewolves, as Bella Swan did, though she is amused when fans ask her – with a straight face – whether she did. Nor was Stephenie invaded by an alien 'soul', as in her novel *The Host*. However, the clues to the plots, themes and characters of her work are written across the childhood of this literary giant. She was born Stephenie Morgan in Hartford, Connecticut, on Christmas Eve, 1973. Some would say it is unfortunate to have a birthday so close to Christmas – and Stephenie would very much agree with them. She groans that her festive-season-timed date of birth 'has always given me a bad attitude to birthdays in general', an attitude that no doubt helped influence the disdain that the *Twilight* heroine Bella Swan feels towards her own birthday, which she expresses in the opening passages of *New Moon*. (Though, as a Virgo, Bella at least avoided having a birthday near Christmas and instead had one in late autumn.)

Stephenie's December date of birth makes her a Capricorn. For those who believe in astrology, Capricorns are said to be creative, sensitive, ambitious and hard-working. These are all qualities that she has shown plenty of in her adult life. She is by no means the only famous scribe born under this sign. Other famous literary Capricorns include fantasy novelist JRR Tolkien, who wrote *The Lord of the Rings* trilogy, and famous authors of other genres including *Catcher in the Rye* writer JD Salinger and Rudyard Kipling, of *Jungle Book* fame. Each of these literary talents tallied with the purported drive for success of the birth sign and achieved enormous appeal, recognition and wealth as their reward. Stephenie would follow gracefully in their footsteps, receiving plenty of those gifts as she did so.

Putting astrology to one side, a perhaps more pertinent – and almost certainly more tangible – effect her date of birth had on Stephenie was that it gave her a place in what has become known as 'Generation Me', or 'the entitlement generation'. A host of respected thinkers in the fields of psychology, sociology and philosophy have written about this trend. They have formed a broad consensus that people born in the

1970s, 1980s and 1990s often exhibit a sharply increased element of narcissism in their personalities. The author Jen M Twenge even published a book called *Generation Me*, which drew on an enormous, authoritative study of more than a million respondents spanning six decades. This trend has been abbreviated as 'GenMe', and those who display its traits have been shown to sink into depression in their late teens and twenties as they accept that their own inflated sense of self-importance is not matched by the adult world at large. However, the impact that her place in 'GenMe' has had most noticeably on Stephenie is seen not through her so much as through her literary characters – particularly Bella Swan. In many ways – not least in her level of loyalty and in the way she marries hard work to her undoubted ambition – Stephenie bucks the 'GenMe' trend, but its characteristics are seen writ large in some of the fictional characters she created, as we shall see.

The first years of her own life were spent in Connecticut, one of America's first states, which was founded in the early 1600s by intrepid Dutch fur traders. It lies in the northeast of the United States, bordered by the states of New York, Massachusetts and Rhode Island. It is the fourth most populated state in America and many of its residents enjoy a high level of prosperity, though it tends towards the Democratic side of the political spectrum. Among other famous Americans to have lived there are the author Mark

Twain, former President George W Bush and film star Meg Ryan.

Connecticut is a rather cold area in winter, but Stephenie would not have to worry about that for long, as the family were to move just a few years into her life. As soon as Stephenie was born that Christmas Eve, her father Stephen and her mother Candy were so proud of her. They decided to name her after her proud father, simply adding two letters to the end of his name to make their newborn daughter's name Stephenie. This slightly unconventional spelling of the name led to a lifetime of frustration for her.

'It drives me mad because it's been spelled wrong all my life,' she has said. Indeed, she nods to this name tweaking in her novel *Breaking Dawn* in the form of a character whose middle name is Carlie. 'Carlie. With a C. Like Carlisle and Charlie put together,' she has said, referring to the first names of two characters from her books.

Stephenie was the second of six children, coming after Emily and before four other Morgan children who followed as the family swelled. She would later describe her family back then as being akin to the famous television clan the Brady Bunch, stars of the sitcom of the same name, which was hugely popular in the 1960s and 1970s. 'I filled the Jan Brady spot in my family,' she has said.

Played by Eve Plumb, Jan was plagued by 'middle child' insecurities. However, the character was more of a painter than a writer and eventually went on to become an architect. Stephenie stops short, though, of comparing her mother to Carol Brady, the mother of the television clan played by Florence Henderson. 'We never had a maid, so my mom is clearly superior to Florence Henderson's character,' she says, 'and also has a better singing voice.'

The family were growing, and so a move was on the cards for the Morgan clan. There was a big change on the horizon for young Stephenie when her father got a new job in his chosen profession of finance. When Stephenie was three years of age, Stephen and Candy decided to move the family to Arizona so he could take up the new post, which was as the chief financial officer, or CFO, with a contracting firm.

Arizona is a far warmer part of America than her birthplace, and Meyer remembers with approval how the move from Connecticut to Arizona meant she was 'transplanted to a more reasonable climate . . . [where they] consider temperatures under seventy-five degrees frigid'.

It was now, once they'd moved to Phoenix, that the two sisters were joined by Heidi, Jacob, Paul and Seth. Stephenie was a caring elder sister, helping out her parents by mucking in with babysitting and nappy-changing duties for her younger siblings.

It is beyond sensible dispute that the large, close family she grew up in had an effect on her fiction.

There are few lonesome characters in her work, for instance. Far more common are characters surrounded by other people, as she always was in her childhood. 'When you grow up in a big family, there's always someone to hang out with,' she says – and always someone to give you ideas for future characters, one could almost add on her behalf. The Morgans also had a dog to complete the wholesome, American family picture. It was called Eagle.

So there was rarely a lonely moment for Stephenie as she grew up, but with such company came a certain neurosis for her. She worried about her brothers frequently, she says. Indeed, when she speaks of them, it is almost as if she were speaking about her own children, not her siblings: 'I used to have mom nightmares about my brothers. When you're a mom you have nightmares about terrible things happening to your kids and you can't stop them. I had those about my brothers.'

Some might say that part of this precocious neurosis was due to her being a Capricorn, who are believed to be people with old heads on young shoulders. (This is a Stephenie preoccupation: in one of her novels, *Breaking Dawn*, her heroine is told by her mother that she was never a teenager and was always older than that in her head.) Later, as she built her own family, she could have drawn on plenty of practice for the worries that plague any mother in the form of those childhood nightmares she had about her brothers and sisters.

Stephenie has always had an overactive imagination in her sleep, not just in a bad way. Later in life a dream would change her life and the face of publishing, when she awoke one summer morning and her life changed for ever.

The Morgans' new family home was on the outskirts of Phoenix in a decidedly suburban area, which Stephenie remembers as being 'free-for-all land'. Accurate words, for, while her neighbours owned horses, the Morgan family built huts and constructed bike paths and a paintball range. Her brothers loved playing war games: '. . . they made [the area] weaponised', she remembered.

Meanwhile, as her brothers' cries of war filled the air outside, Stephenie would be pursuing a far more gentle hobby. She could be found curled up inside the house with her head buried in a book. She describes her teenage self as 'geeky, quiet and book-obsessed'. As such, she found that her place in the family was always clearly set out. 'I was the bookworm,' she says. It was in the blood: both her parents were readers to an extent as well, but it was Stephenie who was the most bookish member of the clan by some distance. She lived for books, particularly novels, and was often to be seen with her head buried in one; and at other times she was read to.

'She was kind of in her own little world,' said her father. 'She would always be making up stories. If she was in a good book, she was perfectly happy off by herself, enmeshing herself in that world.' Despite this interest in books, her parents never predicted that she would become an author. 'We always thought she was going to be a painter,' said her father.

Stephen would often sit in the hallway at night, reading aloud to the children, who lay in their respective bedrooms. A book Stephenie particularly remembers him reading is *The Sword of Shannara*. It was published in 1977, so it would still have been a new affair at the time Stephen read it to the children in the evenings. *The Sword of Shannara* was a big deal as a book at the time, becoming the first fantasy paperback to appear on the *New York Times* bestseller list. It was written by Terry Brooks, who had been influenced by reading JRR Tolkien's classic trilogy *The Lord of the Rings*, which has become an international sensation and a hugely grossing movie series, too. Brooks spent over seven years writing *The Sword of Shannara*, as he was busy studying law at the time. Stephenie would write at a much speedier pace later in life, but the combination of legal studies and fictional writing would echo later in her own life. For now, though, she lay there at night, hearing her father's voice reading from the pages of this fantasy novel, and she felt gripped by the plot and characters. It was always, she emphasises, *Stephen's choice* as to which books he read to them. The book had to interest him, but fortunately she shared his interest in this particular tome. *The Sword of Shannara* is a long book, which interweaves two separate narratives in a fictional world called the Four Lands. It is set 2,000 years after a nuclear holocaust – the 'wars of Ancient Evil' – has taken place and destroyed much of the planet. However, a young boy, half-Elfin and half-human, survives and lives in peace, until a Warlock Lord returns to threaten everything. The only weapon able to keep the evil at bay is a special sword, which must be found for redemption to occur.

It was not exactly comforting bedtime reading, but it was a book that interested Stephen, so that was what the children would listen to at night. And Stephenie wasn't complaining. Eventually, each evening, like all parents, Stephen would decide that was enough reading for the night and would close the book. After wishing them a good night's sleep, he would return to his own business. The children would roll over to sleep, but one of them was rarely satisfied with the amount of the story her father had read them. Stephenie routinely wanted more.

'He always stopped reading when suspense was at its high,' she remembered. The next day, she would rustle through his cupboard and find the book. She would then hide in the cupboard, secretly and silently reading further into the story. She always wanted to know what happened next and wasn't prepared to wait until the next sanctioned evening reading from Stephen. This was not terribly rebellious behaviour from a child, but she could not help but feel she was being naughty during her furtive reading sessions. She remembers 'feeling like I was doing something wrong, like I wasn't supposed to sneak ahead'.

She was hooked, though, by this fantasy story and always needed to know what happened next. But how could she have known, back then, that she would one day write her own novels, which would keep readers – predominantly girls – utterly hooked, too? Millions of girls across the globe have become engrossed in her stories, and snatched every chance they can find to read them.

Her mother, too, had her own literary preferences back in the day. Candy preferred more prim reads, though. These included 19th-century British classics such as those of Jane Austen, whom Meyer loves, too, and has since described as her own 'favourite, favourite' author. She would borrow her mother's books and quickly came to love *Pride And Prejudice*, with its tale of Elizabeth Bennet and Fitzwilliam Darcy. One can almost see the style and form of Stephenie's own novels being shaped right there. Take the fantasy of *The Sword of Shannara*, and add in the romance and troubled relationships of Austen, and you have much of the basis of the *Twilight* series.

'The reason I'm obsessed with the love side of any story is my mom,' she says of her mother's Austen novels. 'I always evaluate a story on relationships and the characters.'

Her parents had formed her interest in stories back

then, and were unintentionally forming the perfect balance for her imagination: the fantasy and romance combination that would underpin the novels she would later write, which would be read by many millions of avid fans.

Among the other books she read and loved were *Gone with the Wind* by Margaret Mitchell and *Jane Eyre* by Charlotte Brontë. 'I read it when I was nine,' says Stephenie of the Brontë classic, 'and I've reread it literally hundreds of times.'

In the process, she became obsessed with the titular character in Brontë's novel, which deals with desire and the complexities of childhood. As she curled up with the book, she immediately connected with the title character of the story. It was a connection that brought her much comfort as she herself dealt with the ups and downs of childhood and then adolescence.

'Jane was someone I was close to as a child,' she says. 'We were good friends! I think in some ways she was more real to me than any other fictional heroine.'

Stephenie's army of fans – many of them teenage girls, of course – speak similarly of the heroine of the *Twilight* series, Bella Swan, who has guided many a troubled teen through her adolescent days. For this reason, Bella could almost be linked to Jane Eyre in a fictional family tree.

It was not just that Stephenie read stories, but she told them too – first to herself. 'I was always a storyteller,' she said in 2006, 'though I only told stories to myself.' Soon, though, her immediate family were being treated to the earliest attempts she made at storytelling, but not on paper. The Morgan family would often drive to visit the grandparents in Utah. They were long journeys, frequently in excess of eight hours, but they were enlivened by Stephenie, who would tell them all stories she had made up in her head. Her imagination would run wild and she would create diverting plots, characters and tales. They may not have been the polished, instant classics she would later create, but they were enough to keep a large family happy during otherwise boring car journeys. Young Stephenie was already showing a definite aptitude for storytelling. Nowadays, kids sit in the backs of cars around the world and read Stephenie's stories to help pass the journey, or listen to the audiobook versions. Others discuss the stories of hers they have already read. Back then, Stephenie's tales on the trips to Utah were often entertaining for the rest of the family.

As a child, she continued to read, and some of her reading was of a more serious nature. Alongside the fantasy novels of her father and the more romantic reads she borrowed from her mother, she also regularly studied a religious tract, *The Book of Mormon*. This is the text of the Latter Day Saint (LDS) movement, whose followers are more commonly known as Mormons.

The Mormon movement was formed in the 19th

century in America. It has since grown into a large international movement with more than 12 million members. Although it believes in and focuses on Jesus Christ, it has a number of differences from the more familiar, mainstream branches of Christianity. Other famous Mormons include Brandon Flowers, lead singer of the Killers, former teen idol Donny Osmond (and many of his family) and *American Idol* pin-up singer David Archuleta, who finished runner-up in the 2008 series and has gone on to considerable commercial success with a string of hits. Stephenie and her parents are Mormons and it was a Mormon household in which she was raised. This has influenced her life and work in many ways, right from when she studied the holy books as a child.

The Book of Mormon, which Stephenie continues to study to this day, was first published in 1830 by Joseph Smith Jr. It is read alongside the Bible by followers, and covers what believers say are tales of God's dealings with ancient dwellers on the American continent. It includes a story of a visitation they claim the resurrected Jesus made to early inhabitants of the land. The book is said to have been translated from hitherto unknown characters, after an angel led Smith to the site of the text, which was inscribed on plates of gold. It is divided into many smaller books, which are read reverentially by followers of the LDS movement. Like all followers, Stephenie has read the books many times. The collective *Book of Mormon* is the tome, she says, 'with the most significant impact on my life'. She reverentially studied the various books within it throughout her childhood.

Her favourite was *The Book of Alma*, which is the longest of all of the books of *The Book of Mormon*. Fully titled *The Book of Alma: The Son of Alma*, it is a 63-chapter epic tale covering missionary work and warfare. Her favourite part of *Alma* comes with the confrontation involving the 2,000 stripling warriors who appear for the first time in *Alma*. The parents of the boys are facing attack but, having converted to Christianity, have promised to not fight. Instead, the children fight to protect the clan and – thanks to their faith – are not injured during the battle. She enjoyed the story a lot growing up, and it helped shape both her faith and her writing.

The influence of the *Alma* story on her own novels would be seen in the future. In addition to the Mormon scriptures, she also read the entire Old Testament once, and has read the New Testament a number of times. A story in the Bible that stood out for Bella is in the book of Kings and involves King Solomon and his reputed wisdom. Two women have rival claims to a baby, each claiming it to be hers. King Solomon calls for the baby to be cut in half and divided between the two women. Naturally, the true mother reveals herself by offering to surrender her claim to a half, in order to ensure that her offspring should live. The sacrifice of the story would ring true for her heroine Bella, and another one of her characters in the *Twilight* series refers to this story as an analogy.

The Mormon atmosphere of the Morgan family demanded that she regularly attend church, study the holy books and live by a number of rules and guidelines set down by the LDS church. If it seems that Stephenie had a somewhat dour childhood, that's because in many ways she did. Certainly, when compared with most kids growing up in the 1970s and 1980s, hers was a sober experience. Pop music, for instance, was strongly discouraged by her parents.

'Actually, growing up, I didn't listen to a ton,' she told *Time* magazine, which is surprising given how important rock music has become to her life in general and her career specifically. 'My parents were pretty strict. I only discovered music as an inspiration later in life.'

Indeed, Stephen and Candy went as far as insisting that any music the children wanted to listen to must be vetted by them first. 'They wanted to listen to everything before we listened to it,' she told *Rolling Stone* magazine, 'so basically we wound up listening to Lionel Richie and Chicago.'

Although she became an author, pop and rock music have become big concerns for Meyer since, influencing her characters and plots. She even used rock concerts as part of the promotional fanfare for one of her novels. Who would have thought that would turn out to be the case during her childhood in the censorious Morgan household?

However, one aspect of Mormonism was to prove very helpful for her in the future. Much of the religion is preoccupied with bringing a proximity between life and death. It must have been some of that imagery that in part influenced Stephenie to write so brilliantly about characters who float between mortality and immortality. The LDS might have had mixed feelings over her vampire stories, but the irony is that it was probably the books of the faith that were hugely influential on the first of her novels, *Twilight*, and its sequels. The evidence is there on the printed page. Indeed, even some of the themes in her adult novel *The Host* can be connected tacitly at least with her Mormon upbringing and beliefs.

Even beyond the sphere of pop music, her cultural input as a teenager was somewhat tame in general for a girl growing up in 1980s America. She was not a fan of horror novels or horror movies. She was, she says, 'a total chicken'. This literary preference remains to this day. 'I've never read a Stephen King book in my life,' she says. 'I just know I'm too much of a wuss for [his] books.' (King would later controversially slam Stephenie's ability as an author, claiming 'she can't write worth a darn'. She responded with dignified silence.) 'I really don't like gore; I hate the slasher type of thing.' As for scary films, 'The most I can handle as far as scary movies [are concerned] is Hitchcock,' she says. 'Anything beyond that, count me out.'

Her favourite film as she grew up was *Somewhere in*

Time, which she watched several times during her youth. Released in 1980, it is a time-travel film with a romantic storyline, adapted from a 1975 novel called *Bid Time Return*, written by Richard Matheson. It concerns a man called Richard Collier, who travels back in time from the 1970s to the 19th century to woo an actress whose photograph had enchanted him. It won the 1976 World Fantasy Award for Best Novel.

The cinematic version was not a huge success commercially or critically, but has built up a substantial cult following, of which Stephenie is a confirmed member. She loved watching it during her teenage years, and enjoyed the performances by *Superman* star Christopher Reeve and Jane Seymour. She also enjoyed the soundtrack, which managed to find its way through Stephen and Candy's vetting procedure.

'The music is Rachmaninoff,' she says. Here she refers to the work of Sergei Rachmaninoff (1873–1943), the Russian-born composer and pianist. His work 'Rhapsody on a Theme of Paganini' is featured in several scenes. It anchored in her imagination the evocative power of music. 'Every time you hear that song,' she said of the soundtrack's lead title, 'you're poised to fall in love. The relationship there is just this impossible thing that he makes possible. That had to be an influence on me.' Indeed it had to be, as anyone who has read her work would instantly understand.

Stephenie also enjoyed watching Saturday-morning television, though she rather shyly describes one of her favourite shows as 'crazy' – the *X-Men* cartoons. This was a series that debuted on Fox in 1992, as part of its Saturday-morning kids' line-up, and it seems she enjoyed it as something of a guilty pleasure. She would happily settle down in front of the latest superhero cartoon and was gripped by the action-packed storylines. 'I was always fascinated with *X-Men*,' she says with a smile. 'I love the idea of a group of people and all of them can do something really well. They're special, but they're strongest when they work together. Maybe that comes from having a big family, but I always clicked into that kind of story.'

Again, the seeds of her later work were being sown in the mind of Stephenie Meyer. *The X-Men* were teaching her a lot about what makes good superhero characters work. That would stand her in great stead in her future career path as one of the most imaginative authors of the modern day.

Many young women get hooked on books and other parts of popular culture such as television and film, but what of the social side of Stephenie's teenage years? Perhaps unsurprisingly, given her quiet bookish nature and strict religious upbringing, Stephenie was a very slow developer when it came to many adolescent rites of passage – not least romance. As she says herself, 'When I was sixteen, holding hands was just – wow!'

It was in a morning church class that she met the boy who became her first boyfriend. Although her hormones may have been racing, she had never been a particularly boy-mad teenager, it was true. In fact, she had something of the tomboy about her. 'My friends used to follow cute boys on the highway,' she said. 'I used to follow cars.'

Later in her life, she would bequeath this motoring passion to one of her own offspring, one of whom boasted from an early age that he knew 'every car in the world'. (Bella Swan, though, is notably ignorant of motoring matters.) As much as any tomboy-ness, her lack of boy chasing had as much to do with her need to behave due to the guidelines and rules laid down by her Mormon faith. 'All of my friends were good girls too,' she explains. 'My boyfriends were good boys.' To a girl growing up around LDS members, this was nothing strange, she says. 'I grew up in a community where it was not the exception to be a good girl. It was sort of expected.' So there was no pressure on her to meet a guy and become sexually experienced.

The boy she met in morning church class was known as KJ. He was not from an especially wealthy background but had many attractive qualities about him. He was several inches taller than Stephenie, who noticed him across the way in the class. The pair quickly became friends and, when it came to the high-school prom, he was the boy she decided to go along with. Prom night is a special experience in the life of any American teenage girl. Stephenie would have been a bit nervous, like most girls. She wore a fetching, knee-length purple dress. KJ wore the customary tuxedo, but topped it off with a bow in the same purple colour as Stephenie's dress.

They sat together at the home of KJ's parents and – slightly nervously – ate a dinner of lemon chicken. They were both very excited and posed holding hands in the family living room. Then they stepped into KJ's father's car – a Mercury Sable, a comfortable mid-size car that KJ had borrowed from his father for the occasion. Some boys hired a limousine for such evenings, but KJ's funds did not run to that. Nor could he afford to have photographs taken by the professional snapper hired at the prom, and the pair were snapped at home instead.

'You're supposed to smile,' the vampire Edward Cullen has to remind Bella in *New Moon* when he takes her photograph. However, both Stephenie and KJ are seen smiling quite naturally in the photographs taken at his house.

It was a memorable evening all round for Stephenie. But, given the way that the awkward Bella of *Twilight* considers the prospect of a school dance at Forks High School in the state of Washington, it is reasonable to assume that Stephenie had not been a natural for the occasion with KJ. Throughout her work, the theme of the prom is one fraught with personal trauma.

Stephenie attended Chaparral High School on East Gold Dust Avenue in Scottsdale, Arizona. She describes the area as 'Arizona's version of Beverly Hills' and compares her high school to the one featured in the film *Clueless*, which is based on the novel *Emma*, by her beloved Jane Austen. The Chaparral High School's mission statement is to develop 'the leaders of tomorrow by providing a safe and respectful educational environment, developing the potential of each individual, encouraging community awareness and fostering a tradition of excellence'. For Meyer, it was a place to study the normal subjects, including English of course. But it was also a place to study those things that dominate everyday life and that are the lifeblood of any novel: characters.

'My focus is the characters,' she says of her writing process, in which the plot is perhaps not given quite as much importance. 'That's the part of the story that is most important to me. I feel the best way to write believable characters is to really believe in them yourself.'

She is at pains to insist that not all her characters are based on real-life people she has met, but admits that is sometimes the case. 'Every now and then there will be a character that is a combination of people I knew. Some of the girls in Bella's high school definitely reflect people I knew at that stage in my life,' she said.

Her circle of friends represented a fairly varied bunch of characters. 'It was me, the crazy Mormon . . . the hippie-raised atheist, the Jewish girl, the Baptist and then the quiet Lutheran,' she remembers. 'We had some pretty mind-boggling religious discussions.' The one person who was missing from her circle of friends had yet to be created – Bella Swan, heroine of the *Twilight* series. Stephenie would have appreciated such a friend in her circle back then. 'I wish I would have known someone like her when I was seventeen,' said Stephenie. 'She would have been a good person to be friends with.'

Stephenie sees similarities between Swan and her own teenage self. 'I think she has a few things in common with [me],' she says. 'The same shyness and wobbly self-confidence, and a few physical similarities.'

Despite her relationship with KJ, she recalls herself as a retiring pupil who was not overly popular with the boys. 'In high school, I was a mousy, A-track wallflower. I had a lot of incredible girlfriends, but I wasn't much sought after by the Y chromosomes, if you know what I mean,' she says.

A teacher from the school concurs with Stephenie's self-assessment. 'She was bright but not overly so,' says Conrad Davis, her former English teacher. 'Her writing was good but not outstanding. I remember her being very polite and fairly shy. She was from a Mormon family and those girls were always the best behaved in school. Stephenie was a good girl. We did the usual high-school studies – Shakespeare, American literature and some of the English writers such as Jane Austen. Stephenie was in my daughter's year but when she became famous both of us had to look her picture up to remember her clearly. She just blended in.'

In blending in, she did not find enormous amounts

of happiness, and this was not a period of her life she recalls with much fondness. 'Don't ever let anyone tell you that high school is supposed to be fun,' she wrote. 'High school is to be endured.' She really was a quiet, non-intrusive personality in her high-school days. 'I was practically Cousin Itt in high school,' she says, referring humorously to the character in television show *The Addams Family* who is covered head to toe in hair. 'You know, hair in the face, hide from everyone.'

Books, as ever, were her salvation during these testing times. 'I kind of read in my room all the time. I read the fattest books I could get my hands on. Every Wednesday was library day. I checked [the *Anne of Green Gables* series] out every week. I practically owned them.'

That said, with the passage of time, she later spoke more favourably of her school years. 'It wasn't too torturous,' she said. 'I had a little niche with the advanced students and an eclectic, warm circle of friends. I was very shy, so I was quiet in class and made no waves. English and art were my favourite subjects.'

She also gained inspiration for characters from closer to home, where, as we have seen, the size of the Morgan family again came in handy. 'I think that coming from such a large family has given me a lot of insight into different personality types – my siblings sometimes crop up as characters in my stories.'

However, she was about to move away from home,

as it was time for her to start her university education. Although she was being sent to an establishment that was approved by the Mormon movement, this move away from the clutches of her parents would see her life change in many ways. She was not about to go wild, it was true, but the girl who had been a 'wallflower' at school was about to begin to bloom, and would begin to freely try some of the fruits that were forbidden her back home.

She liked what she tasted.

chapter two
university challenges

Stephenie Meyer had been at Chaparral High School for four years when she moved to a new educational establishment. She enrolled at the Brigham Young University (BYU) in Provo, Utah. This is a privately owned institution, established in 1875 by the then president of the LDS, Brigham Young. He laid down the blueprint for the university's educational approach when he told a colleague succinctly, 'I want you to remember that you ought not to teach even the alphabet or the multiplication tables without the Spirit of God.'

It was originally a school, rather than a university. It is owned by the Church of the Latter Day Saints and around 98 per cent of its students are Mormons. Most students and alumni refer to it as 'The Lord's University'. Stephenie was not about to easily experience the sort of sexual promiscuity or alcohol-drenched social life of many university students, as dramatised in books such as *I Am Charlotte Simmons* by Tom Wolfe. Instead, she was expected to conform to the strict codes of behaviour expected of the BYU students. There is even a pocket-sized booklet titled 'For the Strength of Youth' that is handed to students, which outlines the code of conduct that they would need to abide by. One edition of the pamphlet has a cover image of four wholesome-looking smiling American teens (two girls, two boys) and contains a series of proscriptions regarding student conduct, an awkward-looking neologism and the occasional bizarre use of exclamation marks to boot. It is remarkable to think of a university student in the modern age being given such strict rules.

It begins with a message from the 'Presidency' of the LDS, addressed to 'our beloved young men and women'. The introduction continues, 'You cannot do wrong and feel right. It is impossible! Years of happiness can be lost in the foolish gratification of a momentary desire for pleasure.' The section promises students that those who conform to the required behaviour will, among other things, be rewarded with 'the constant and calming companionship of the Holy Ghost'.

The following section informs the youth of the LDS that 'Your entire lives on earth are intended to give you the opportunity to learn to choose good over evil, service over selfishness, kindness and thoughtfulness over self-indulgence and personal gratification.' Among the rules laid down about personal relationships are that students should not date until they are 16 years of age, and that they must go on double or group dates only.

'Plan positive and constructive activities when you are together,' it tells daters. The pamphlet also orders chastity before marriage and bans homosexuality. However, it assures concerned readers, 'Victims of rape, incest, or other sexual abuse are not guilty of sin. If you have been a victim of any of these terrible crimes, be assured that God still loves you!'

In a section called 'Friendshipping', Mormon youngsters are given guidelines on how to choose, interact with and treat their friends. 'If some of your friends are shy and do not feel included, be particularly sensitive to their feelings and go out of your way to pull them into the influence of your strong circle of good friends,' it implores kindly – though the text takes a more predatory turn when it encourages youngsters to recruit new members to the LDS church. 'Invite your nonmember friends to Church activities where they can learn about your standards and the principles of the gospel,' it says.

'Include them in your midweek activities and your Sunday meetings. Help them feel welcome and wanted. Many non-members have come into the Church through friends who have involved them in Church activities.'

The pamphlet also counsels students to dress modestly and resist fashion. 'If you wear an immodest bathing suit because it's "the style," it sends a message that you are using your body to get attention and approval,' it says.

Stephenie, along with the other young women of the LDS, were told to 'refrain from wearing off-the-shoulder, low-cut, or revealing clothes'. She had never really been a provocative dresser, but how much of that was down to her inherent nature and how much had to do with the pressure of the LDS is hard to ascertain. She would have noticed among the males of the university that they were clean-shaven, and that their hair did not grow over the ear and that any sideburns they had did not extend beyond the earlobe or cheek. Again, this was as a result of university rules that covered even the style and length of the head hair and facial hair that male students were expected to follow.

After a section encouraging students to avoid dishonesty or bad language, they are also warned against gossip, which is described as 'another kind of harmful language. When you say something bad about people who are not present or tell secrets you know about them, you are gossiping. Gossip causes hurt and pain for other people.'

If that would seem to run contrary to the behaviour of students across the world, so does the rule that no student must work on the sabbath, be that college work or a part-time job. With the pressures of their studies to keep up with and funds as ever short, this banning of any work on Sundays put extra pressure on the student body.

Even how they relaxed on the sabbath was subject to rules and restrictions. 'You should avoid seeking entertainment or spending money on this day,' it says. Drinking alcohol is out not just on the sabbath, but every day. It is not the only substance banned, either. 'Hard drugs, wrongful use of prescription drugs, alcohol, coffee, tea, and tobacco products – such as cigarettes, snuff, chewing tobacco, cigars, and pipe tobacco – destroy your physical, mental, and spiritual well-being. Tobacco can enslave you, weaken your lungs, and shorten your life. Any form of alcohol, including beer, is harmful to your spirit and your body. Drinking will dull your conscience, is expensive, and could lead to alcoholism, which is self-destructive, dangerous, and deadly.'

Even among those social activities that are not banned outright, the pamphlet encourages constant vigilance from its readers. 'Don't be afraid to walk out of a movie, turn off a television set, or change a radio station if what's being presented does not meet your Heavenly Father's standards. And do not read books or magazines or look at pictures that are pornographic or that present immorality as acceptable. In short, if you have any question about whether a particular movie, book, or other form of entertainment is appropriate, don't see it, don't read it, don't participate.'

As for music, which Stephenie had also encountered restrictions on, the booklet says, 'You should be willing to control your listening habits and shun music that is spiritually harmful. Don't listen to music that contains ideas that contradict principles of the gospel.'

As we shall see, Stephenie fell in love with rock music during her university years as she finally broke free from the prim clutches of her parents and their musical rules. It is unlikely that the LDS would have approved of all that she listened to, as she became enthralled by quite heavy rock sounds.

And so this strange publication comes to a resounding climax. 'Always take a stand for the Lord's way,' concludes the main body of the pamphlet, 'he has promised to help you as you live gospel standards.' The final page lists the rules in bullet-point form, to reinforce the messages and to allow a quick check for any confused student. While the rules in the pamphlet were not enforced with brutal or savage strictness, it was very much expected that students would abide by them.

Moving away to university can be a difficult experience for any young person. While the rules outlined may have complicated the experience in some ways for Stephenie, in others they may have offered a moral framework that made her choices during her university years easier to negotiate, and at least the majority of the student body were following the guidelines, so she was surrounded by people who related to her. Certainly, she abided by many of guidelines and rules. Others, though, including the strict guidelines about rock music, she was happy to interpret in the way that suited her.

She kept to the sexual guidelines and this fact would benefit her further down the line, in that it encouraged the LDS to support her novels, where it might just as easily have turned on a member writing about vampires of all things. Of course, all that restraint she showed fuelled the vivid way she represented just that quality in her novels. She did, though, regularly date. Students were encouraged to keep the pamphlet with them at all times, and nowadays it has a web presence too, including a Facebook page devoted to both the pamphlet and its teachings.

It is not just the students who have to live under rules and guidelines laid down by the LDS: the teaching staff do, too. In 1992, a 'Statement on Academic Freedom' arguably contradicted its title when it severely limited what statements lecturers were allowed to make during classes. Specifically, it banned 'Expression with students or in public that: (1) contradicts or opposes, rather than analyzes or discusses, fundamental Church doctrine or policy; (2) deliberately attacks or derides the Church or its general leaders; or (3) violates the Honor Code because the expression is dishonest, illegal, unchaste, profane, or unduly disrespectful of others.' In the wake of this controversial move, several lecturers have faced disciplinary action as a result of their perceived infringements of these rules. Although it is perfectly legal for a religious educational establishment to limit academic freedom as long as it does so openly, BYU has faced criticism from the American Association of University Professors, which alleged that 'infringements on academic freedom are distressingly common and that the climate for academic freedom is distressingly poor' at BYU.

Whatever the accuracy of that indictment, back then Stephenie lived under the strict rules of the establishment and therefore had a copy of the guideline pamphlet with her during her university years. It certainly influenced her experiences at BYU. To secure a place at the university, she – like all prospective students – had to provide a reference from a religious leader. The sexually promiscuous, alcohol-ridden, drug-experimenting riotous university experience was not one that she went through. In fact, it is worth pausing to examine exactly what being a Mormon means for Stephenie's day-to-day life. It means she does not drink alcohol or take drugs and even avoids caffeine. (Bella, the heroine of the *Twilight* series, has a low tolerance to caffeine.) She has been known to waver slightly on caffeine, occasionally indulging in a diet-soda drink, which might include a tiny amount of the stuff.

'It's about keeping yourself free of addictions,' she says, explaining the thinking behind the rule. 'We have free will, which is a huge gift from God. If you tie that up with something like, I don't know, cocaine, then you don't really have a lot of freedom any more.'

It was perhaps in the area of sexuality that the Mormon teachings had the biggest impact on Stephenie during her university years. Although it may not have seemed strange at the Mormon-dominated BYU for her to not be experimenting sexually, set against the experiences of young women her age at other colleges, her abstinence was less than common. This means that in a key area of her development as a young woman she was standing outside the experiences of many her age. This gave her an increasingly rarefied insight into qualities – such as restraint – that would serve her well later in life.

Off she went to university, though, having kissed her mother and father goodbye, with her Mormon pamphlet packed along with the usual student paraphernalia. She had been awarded a National Merit Scholarship, which helped fund her studies. This was recognition of the hard work she had put in at Chaparral High School and is an honour of some distinction for any student to receive. Over a million students apply for the scholarship each year and only a fraction are granted it. The purpose of it is 'to identify and honor academically talented US high school students, to stimulate increased support for their education, and to provide efficient and effective scholarship program management for organizations that wish to sponsor college undergraduate scholarships'.

She studied English Literature at BYU. This had been an easy choice for the bookworm girl to make. 'I don't know if I ever considered anything else. That's what I love. I love reading, and this was a major I could read in,' she says. 'I figured I'd go on and go to law school, but I wasn't super-concerned with supporting myself because I wasn't thinking beyond being a student.'

It was when she went to university that her love of rock and pop music took off. Freed from the clutches of her censorious parents, she began to listen to more and more rock music. During her free time, she had what could only be described as a crash course in rock and pop music. She liked what she heard. Her favourite band is Muse, who 'are the common denominator in all my MP3 playlists', she says.

Muse are a three-piece rock band formed in Devon in 1994. Their five studio albums mix a variety of musical genres, including prog rock, classic and electro music. The vocals are often delivered in falsetto, leading to comparisons between Muse and classic rock bands such as Queen, whose guitarist Brian May is a fan, calling Muse 'extraordinary musicians'.

She also became a fan of My Chemical Romance, Linkin Park and Coldplay. My Chemical Romance are a five-piece emo rock band from New Jersey, best known for their operatic rock style as evinced in their hit 'The Black Parade'. Linkin Park – a six-piece from California – merge nu metal and rap-rock influences into an enormously successful sound that has become the soundtrack to the lives of numerous people – including Stephenie and many of her teenage fans. Formed in London in 1998, Coldplay are a far more tranquil affair. Their songs are melodic, almost meditative, and firmly at the 'easy listening' end of the rock spectrum. As such they are probably the band who least test the boundaries of the Mormon directives.

These were the kinds of sounds Stephenie was listening to, once her parents' restrictions were removed from her day-to-day life. She also wrote some 'really bad poetry' while at college. Music and poetry were not the only ways in which she began to emerge a bit from the prim shadow that the LDS cast over her childhood. At university, she remembered, her level of attractiveness to boys soared. She had not noticed much interest from boys in her at high school, but all that was to change with the move to Utah.

'Let me tell you, my stock went through the roof,' she said. 'See, beauty is a lot more subjective than you might think. In Scottsdale, surrounded by barbies, I

35

was about a five. In Provo, surrounded by normal people, I was more like an eight. I had dates every weekend with lots of really pretty and intelligent boys, some of whose names end up in my books. It was quite confusing at first, because I knew there was nothing different about me.' Instead, it was those surrounding her who had changed. She had seemed a 'wallflower' at school when compared with classmates of more provocative appearance. The more demure appearances of the BYU female students pushed her further into the radar of the males.

They liked what they saw and she was happy to date them, while always maintaining a chaste lifestyle, as was expected of her until marriage.

'I didn't date very much at all in high school,' she confirmed. 'When I got to college, most of my relationships were light-hearted and very brief. It was a joke with my roommates that I never dated anyone longer than two weeks unless I was engaged to him.' (She remains, in her own mind at least, a tame character. She was once asked what a burger to be named in her honour should be like. 'The Stephenie should be the name for the plainest burger you have,' she replied.)

A friend from her schooldays believes that any guys Stephenie dated during this period would not have got to know her very well. 'I don't think she ever had a proper boyfriend. When she came back from college she and Pancho got together and then the next thing I heard they were married. I think he's probably the only man she's been with.'

And here is where 'Pancho' enters the narrative of young Stephenie Morgan's life, for she would soon re-encounter a figure from her childhood who would go on to become her husband. She had first met Christiaan Meyer as a child, shortly after her family moved to Arizona. This being real life rather than a novel, it was not exactly love at first sight. 'We didn't like each other at all,' she says of her early encounters with Christiaan. 'He was part of a different crowd and some of his friends were kind of mean.'

He had been nicknamed Pancho by his grandmother and continues to be called that to this day, including on the Acknowledgements page of *Twilight*. However, it would not be until a little later in her life that their paths would cross again and their relationship would take a different turn. It was when she was 20 years old and at BYU that she and Pancho started dating. 'We saw each other again, and we'd both changed a little bit,' she says of their reuniting proper – changed for the better, in her eyes. He looks good, she thought when she saw him. Their paths had crossed regularly in the meantime, at church events and social functions. However, it was not until they were both in their twenties that their relationship restarted and turned towards the romantic.

That said, due to her religion, it is safe to assume that the relationship will not have been consummated until after marriage. As she herself said, the young people of her religion are always in a hurry to marry for that precise reason. Pancho actually proposed to her on their second date, but Stephenie dashed his hopes when she said no. However, he was persistent – and he had to be. She actually estimates that he proposed 40 times before she finally said yes. 'He would propose every night,' she said with a smile, 'and I would tell him no every night. It was kind of our end-of-date thing.'

It must have been frustrating for Pancho, but quite possibly amusing for Stephenie, particularly if she had already decided she would eventually say yes. Finally, she actually did say yes and they married in 1994 – just nine months after their first date. Her husband is a man for whom she feels enormous love and respect, naturally. She believes that his mother was a key figure in shaping him into the man she so admires and appreciates. 'He expects the women in his life to have interests and opinions and a mind of her own,' she says approvingly. 'He can handle the fact that I am at least as strong a person as he is, and that I am smart and capable and often right.' He can also handle her at times rather direct humour – which is lucky. 'My saddest day was when I had to move out of an apartment with six girls and move in with my husband,' she joked during an interview.

Three years after she married, Stephenie graduated with her bachelor's degree in English Literature. She would later become a famous member of the BYU alumni, which also includes politician Mitt Romney; Nobel prizewinner Paul D Boyer; co-inventor of the television Philo Farnsworth; Jon Heder, who played the title role in the 2004 cult smash film *Napoleon Dynamite*; and Golden Globe-nominated actor Aaron Eckhart.

Heder is a particularly notable example because his role as Napoleon Dynamite was, say some commentators, influenced in part by his Mormon background, which was shared by some of the filmmakers. The film focused on the titular hero, a gawky, nerdy kid who lives with his grandmother and elder brother in Preston, Idaho, together with their llama. Dynamite is a hilarious character who wears T-shirts tucked deep into waist-high jeans, black moon boots and steel-rimmed glasses. He has an eminently quotable vocabulary, including a battalion of inoffensive curse words such as 'Dang!' and 'Gosh!' As the film progresses, Napoleon's comic uncle arrives to look after them and Napoleon then befriends Pedro, a new kid at school who rivals him for awkwardness. The film ends with Pedro, against all odds, winning the class presidency.

As we shall see, much discussion has taken place over whether Stephenie's writing and the subsequent films are influenced by or representative of her

Mormon faith. For many observers and one filmmaker, there is no doubt about a connection between Mormonism and *Napoleon Dynamite*, even though no character in the film is explicitly connected with the faith in any way.

'I think that [Mormons] definitely see some correlation between the Napoleon character coming up with creative alternatives to swearwords like "Gosh!", "Dang!" and "Frickin' idiot!",' says Jared Hess, who befriended Heder at BYU and directed *Napoleon Dynamite*. 'In Mormon households, that's what kids have to do.'

Stephenie is clearly a fan of the wacky cult film – in a family photograph taken of her three young sons one Hallowe'en, one of them was dressed as Napoleon Dynamite – and, although she has never publicly commented on the film, certainly her own characters stop short of obscene language, as does Dynamite, so the Mormon-influence theory is plausible. Robert Kirby, the *Salt Lake Tribune* journalist and author of several humorous Mormon books, certainly believes so. '[Heder] promises real hope for the way Mormons are regarded in film,' he says. 'What we're looking for is our own stereotype. And, without doing it in an overt or in-your-face way, he brings the Mormon character to the screen.'

The Mormon influence on Stephenie's writing is by no means overt – how could a story about vampires and lust be so? However, as we shall see, there is an undercurrent throughout the stories of religious influence. Stephenie's writing is in no way dominated or dependent on her Mormonism, though. The year that Stephenie graduated from BYU, a book was being published in the United Kingdom that would change the face of publishing for young people and pave the way for Stephenie's success the following decade.

JK Rowling wrote the book on a manual typewriter. It had been a difficult process to completion for Rowling, who was struck by inspiration on a long train journey but had no means to write down her thoughts. Then, as she sat writing the book on her old typewriter day in, day out, tragedy struck. Rowling's mother died at just 45 years of age. In response, she felt compelled to get away from everything and moved to Portugal to teach English. She took her typewriter and wrote a chapter – her favourite of the book – while there. By the time she returned to England, Rowling had a daughter, Jessica, to look after. Whenever her child fell asleep, Rowling would write as much as she could during the peaceful time. She particularly enjoyed writing in cafés so she would not have to stop for long in order to refuel with coffee. She was battling depression at the time, but the story she was putting together would place a smile on the faces of readers across the globe.

The resulting work, *Harry Potter and the Philosopher's Stone*, was a fantasy novel about a teenage wizard. It was finally published in 1997, as Stephenie was graduating from BYU over in America. The book went on to become a runaway success very quickly indeed, winning awards and topping the bestseller lists within months of its hitting the shelves. By the time subsequent titles in the seven-book series were published, millions of copies were being snapped up in the first few hours of publication and the story had been adapted into a blockbusting movie series.

Rowling is more than halfway to being a billionaire now; according to some reports, she is even wealthier than Queen Elizabeth II. Without this trailblazing success for the *Harry Potter* series, Stephenie might not have found it so easy to pursue her own writing career, nor might it have been such an attractive prospect for her. The *Potter* books had reignited children's interest in reading and left publishers around the world desperate to sign their own Rowling, who could write them stories that would sell millions of copies to the kids who were flocking to bookshops again. Where might they find such a person?

Stephenie was just a few years off bringing her own characters to the big screen, but few could have known it in the immediate wake of her graduation from BYU. While Pancho went out to work each day, she became a 'stay-at-home mom' and prepared to raise her new family. While she was very much a proud, happy mother, one wonders whether a part of her regretted marrying so soon after graduation.

Certainly, in her books, there are regular suggestions that this could be the case. In her novel *Eclipse*, for instance – the third novel in the *Twilight* series – her heroine Bella speaks with disdain of how her mother married straight after leaving high school, describing that decision as 'a life-altering mistake'. She says with disgust that her mother's action was 'thoughtless and goofy' and ruminates that 'smart people' make sure they develop a career and experience more of life before settling down.

Nor does she leave her harsh verdict there. Bella later sneeringly describes an archetypal 'small-town hick' who gets 'married right out of high school'. She rages, 'I wasn't going to be that girl! That's not who I am!' There's more: later in the novel, Edward's love rival Jacob Black urges Bella to not settle down too fast. 'Think about it, Bella. According to you, you've kissed just one person . . . in your whole life, and you're calling it quits? How do you know that's what you want? Shouldn't you play the field a little?'

Is Stephenie speaking to herself through these characters? While she remains a loving and faithful wife, is there a part of her psyche jumping out of the page at us here?

Playing the field, though, was the opposite of what Stephenie did – although, unlike the mother in *Eclipse*, she at least had her university years to enjoy and experience before she tied the knot. She suffered some upsets during this time after break-ups with men, but she denies that such moments helped fuel her ability to write about Bella's pain. 'I have never suffered a heartbreak like Bella's,' she says. 'Nothing close. The few times I had my heart stepped on, I was not devastated, nor was I melodramatic. Life went on, and I went with it. I was very practical about my rejections, and I was well aware that it was never true love that I was losing.' She had found true love with Pancho, though, and it was then time to stay at home and begin to build her own family.

The first member appeared two years after she and Pancho married, when she gave birth to their first son, Gabe, in 1998. Four years later, another son, Seth, followed and then a year later Eli came. 'They're perfect,' says the doting, loving mother of her three sons. She has no immediate plans to add to the family now, but jokes that, in the wake of her teen-girl-dominated *Twilight* fanbase appearing, she has considered adopting a teenage daughter. Indeed, she had a name lined up for a daughter but never got to award it – until she gave it to the heroine of her first novel, as we shall see.

Stephenie has taken to motherhood excellently and has an easily expressed grasp of what the role entails. 'Everybody's somebody's kid, right? So, as a mom, compassion comes with the territory. You want people to be happy; you want to understand them; you want them to be well adjusted.'

With motherhood, though, there also came the

dawning of a whole new weight of responsibility. She found that the sorts of nightmare she had as a child, when she had worried in her sleep about her younger siblings, came back as she was plagued by further bad dreams. But this time they were even more distressing because they focused on her own children. As Bella protests in *New Moon*, 'If I close my eyes now, I'll see things I don't want to see. I'll have nightmares.' Sleeping fantasies loom large in the life story of Stephenie.

While Pancho went to work each day as an auditor for an accountancy firm, she stayed at home and raised the children. She had done some work as a receptionist, but was very much settling into the stay-at-home-mum role. There were few clues at this stage as to what fate had in store for her, and little sign of the enormous creativity she was to show. While at college, she had written a bit of the aforementioned 'bad poetry' and done a spot of painting from time to time. Prior to the arrival of Gabe, she had written a few chapters of some unnamed stories, but since he came into the world she had not done any writing whatsoever. She feared that writing fiction would allow others to get inside her head, somewhere she was not at this stage keen for anyone to be. Writing was one of those indulgences that were quickly forgotten once the realities of parenthood dawned on her. Indeed, after she had graduated, one of the most creative things she did with her time was occasional visits to a scrapbook club. (Her *Twilight* heroine Bella is given a scrapbook for her 18th birthday in the second instalment of the series, *New Moon*.) That was one of the only times Stephenie left the family home to do something for her own pleasure in those days, though she went to the cinema quite a bit, too.

She was more often seen at home, though, doing mother stuff. She would change nappies, bathe the kids, read them stories, stitch Hallowe'en outfits for them. Then there was the ever-present backdrop of church activities for her to immerse herself in. It was a happy existence, but one that lacked any considerable deviation from the norm. Women like her existed across America; their lives and contributions were entirely admirable, content and tranquil. Few of them, however, would break out of their existence to do anything like Stephenie did.

The clue to her amazing future was actually obvious, though, to those closer to her home – with the benefit of hindsight at least. As she sat with her successive babies in her arms, her free hand always had the same thing in it – a book. She may have given up her writing in the face of motherhood, but she read as much as, if not more than, she did before. She devoured novels by a range of different authors from a wide variety of genres. The great English bard William Shakespeare, including his classic *Romeo & Juliet*; the Canadian author of *Anne of Green Gables* and subsequent Anne Shirley novels, LM Montgomery, who is her favourite young-adult author; the 19th-century American writer Louisa May Alcott; the American science-fiction novelist Orson Scott Card; Janet Evanovich, who began her own writing career penning romance novels and moved on to the mystery genre – all of these Stephenie loved to read. Evanovich would, soon enough, be the catalyst for Stephenie's own catapulting into literary fame on a practical level.

Meanwhile, she was becoming ever more the bookworm and soaking up the craft of putting together a fantastic, engrossing read. Indeed, during her course at BYU, she preferred reading to writing. For her, it was exciting that something she enjoyed doing anyway could be considered 'work' in the educational sense. She remains a fan of other authors, and says she dreams of witnessing a panel discussion between Orson Scott Card, William Shakespeare and Jane Austen. Only the truly bookish could have such fantasies. Perhaps here, too, we see a touch of her tomboy ways. Imagining such line-ups is a rather male pursuit, is it not?

Of *Anne of Green Gables* she is particularly gushing in her admiring words. Published in 1908, it is the story of a couple who adopt a child, but, rather than the boy they expected, they are presented with a feisty, entertaining and creative girl. A story that is at turns funny and moving, it is a true classic that has been adapted for film, too. Stephenie liked the

47

longevity of the narrative particularly. 'I was never a fan of the stories where everything ends and they kiss at the wedding,' she said. '*Anne of Green Gables* started out with her as a child. She had a very fully described adolescence; she had a book-long engagement; we got to see her wedding; we got to see her have her first child and lose her first child; we got to see her children grow up. We got the whole life, and I loved that.'

Her character Bella, in the *Twilight* series, mentions *Green Gables* on several occasions, particularly during *Eclipse*, the third novel in the series. When she imagines marrying Edward, the dashing *Twilight* hero, she keeps having what she describes as '*Green Gables* flashbacks'.

Stephenie considers *Speaker for the Dead* by the aforementioned Orson Scott Card the most influential novel on her career. The hero of the science-fiction novel is Ender Wiggin, who in a previous novel in the series (*Ender's Race*) had wiped out an alien race – 'the buggers'. *Speaker for the Dead* is set in 5270, 3,000 years after the first instalment. Ender declares that this was a mistake, and yearns for atonement. When a second alien race – known as 'the piggies' – emerges, he has his chance to bring it about. In a lengthy and ambitious novel, themes of a cultural and religious nature are covered. It was a success when published in 1986, winning the Nebula Award. It followed that by scooping the Hugo Award the following year.

Perhaps the most prestigious honour it has received, however, is Meyer's endorsement of it as the most influential novel on her as a writer. 'The romances are a small part of his books, but they bring his people to life,' she purred. Two decades after it was first published, *Speaker for the Dead* began to sell like hotcakes off the back of her praise for it. She ranks its author, Card, as the person she would most like to have dinner with. 'I have a million questions for him. Mostly things like, "How do you come up with this stuff?"'

They would have plenty to discuss, for he too has history with the LDS church, and served a mission for the Church in Brazil during the early 1970s. He has since become a politically controversial figure who has campaigned against gay rights and in support of the foreign policy of the George W Bush administration. However, she remains a fan. 'He's sort of my favourite writer who's alive,' she says. She includes a quote from his book *Empire* in the introduction to one of the chapters in the fourth book in the *Twilight* series, *Breaking Dawn*.

Other authors she is on the record as admiring are Daphne du Maurier, who wrote the big-screen-adapted stories *The Birds*, *Don't Look Now* and *Rebecca*. She also read some of the epic fantasy works of David Eddings, the murder mysteries of Agatha Christie, *The Princess Bride* by William Goldman and *A Company of Swans* by Eva Ibbotson.

Having left university, she was no less inclined to read novels of all kinds – it became a standing joke in the Meyer household. 'I just read all the time,' she said. 'In fact, my husband used to tease me. I went through six years of always having a little baby in my arms, and so my other hand was pretty much shaped in the form of a book to hold it open. I probably read five to six novels a week.'

One type of novel that Stephenie did *not* read, though, was anything to do with vampires. The closest she came was to reading a couple of novels by Anne Rice, whose canon of Gothic-themed books include some vampire themes. Curious, no? In any case, reading at a rate of almost one novel per day, she was – consciously or subconsciously – absorbing the tricks of the trade at an astonishing rate. Ostensibly, the novels were keeping her company as she stayed at home looking after the kids while Pancho was out at work. When she created her own characters, she infused one of them with a love of books. 'Don't you know it by heart yet?' asked Edward of Bella as she sat reading *Wuthering Heights* for the umpteenth time in a conversation that could have originally taken place in the Meyer household.

'You have some serious issues with the classics,' Bella snaps back.

Some mothers vegetate in front of daytime television during any breaks they get from the demanding job of motherhood, and there's nothing wrong with that. For Stephenie, though, it was books that did the trick, getting her through long, tiring days as a young mother. They were tiring because the children were energetic. She has said that her young boys remind her of 'chimpanzees on crack'. She was a loving mother but, like most mums, frequently a tired one too. The books became her escape, the characters her friends. She awoke each morning with endless, tiresome domestic tasks ahead of her. They were often mundane days but she always had the prospect of more reading, which could transport her to different places and different worlds. She really wore the books down physically, prompting, in the novel she would write, an aside about the book a character is reading being so worn down that it slumped flat on the table when she put it down. Plenty of *Twilight* fans would relate to this.

As we have seen and shall see again, reading was more than just a leisure activity with an element of escape. Stephenie was laying the foundations in her own imagination for how to produce her own writing. 'Reading was really my only training in fiction writing,' she says. 'I never took a class or read a book on how to write. I just absorbed the basics from reading thousands of other people's stories.' Soon, she would start writing a story herself – one that would transport millions of engrossed, delighted fans to a different place.

She went to bed one night, switching off the light and sinking into the mattress as she closed her eyes. Sleep came upon her. Life would never be the same again.

chapter three
a wonderful dream

Stephenie Meyer can pinpoint the exact date that she was struck with the inspiration for the *Twilight* series. It was the first day that her children took swimming lessons and she began her summer diet, and therefore the date was marked on her calendar: it was 2 June 2003. The summer was proving a somewhat testing one for Stephenie and Pancho. When she was pregnant with Eli, she had fallen over and broken her arm badly. As she was an expectant mother, the accident caused enormous concern for her and Pancho particularly since during her first pregnancy she had been mistakenly warned that a miscarriage was imminent.

The worry was not finished, because, just over a month later, Pancho was diagnosed with Crohn's disease, a condition that causes a painful inflammation of the intestines. Difficult treatment ensued, and all this

53

caused yet more worry and pain for both of them. Amid all this stress, and in the wake of her successive pregnancies, Stephenie had put on a lot of weight and she was facing a significant birthday at the end of the year, too. Never a fan of birthdays, because hers falls so close to Christmas, she was even less enthusiastic than normal for another reason: it was another milestone on the way to old age. No wonder she felt rather unhappy with her lot. 'It wasn't a great time in my life,' she said. 'My thirtieth birthday was coming up and I was so not ready to face being thirty,' she says. 'I didn't feel I had much going for me. I had my kids, but there wasn't much I was doing.'

All that was about to change on the evening of 1 June 2003. She was about to have a great deal going for her, and getting there was going to keep her very busy indeed. That evening she experienced the most vivid and powerful dream in her sleep. It was truly haunting. She dreamed the most odd scenario.

'In my dream, two people were having an intense conversation in a meadow in the woods,' she explained on her official website. 'One of these people was just your average girl. The other person was fantastically beautiful, sparkly, and a vampire. They were discussing the difficulties inherent in the facts that . . . they were falling in love with each other while . . . the vampire was particularly attracted to the scent of her blood, and was having a difficult time restraining himself from killing her immediately.'

Then, as often seems to happen with intense dreams, she suddenly woke up. She awoke at 4 a.m. haunted by the images and scenario that had come to her in her sleep. 'It was very clear. I was an observer. When I woke up, I sat there with my eyes closed, thinking about it,' she says. 'It was like reading a great book when you don't want to put it down. You want to know what happens next. So, I just lay there imagining what I had seen in my sleep.' She was gripped (and was in effect watching in her mind the first screen adaptation of *Twilight*).

Parental duties were put on hold for a little while. She wanted to stay right where she was and keep going over the scene in her mind. 'Though I had a million things to do – i.e. making breakfast for hungry children, dressing and changing the diapers of said children, finding the swimsuits that no one ever puts away in the right place, et cetera – I stayed in bed, thinking about the dream,' she has said.

A dutiful, responsible mother, she was nonetheless temporarily almost stunned by the dream and its aftermath. Just as the dream haunted her for the moment, so did the very real sense that she might quickly lose her memory of it. 'I was so intrigued by the nameless couple's story that I hated the idea of forgetting it; it was the kind of dream that makes you want to call your friend and bore her with a detailed description. Also, the vampire was just so darned good-looking that I didn't want to lose the mental image.

'Unwillingly, I eventually got up and did the immediate necessities, and then put everything that I possibly could on the back burner and sat down at the computer to write – something I hadn't done in so long that I wondered why I was bothering. But I didn't want to lose the dream, so I typed out as much as I could remember, calling the characters "he" and "she".'

Joking that becoming the mother of three kids brought on 'early Alzheimer's', she decided to write the details down before they slipped from her memory. She opened a new document on her computer and began to type. The first line she wrote was: 'In the sunlight, he was shocking.' *Twilight* was under way.

His very existence in her imagination was shocking, too. For, as we have seen, Stephenie was no fan of vampire books or films. So it is strange that she dreamed so vividly of a vampire, and that the imagery so appealed to her.

'That's the weirdest thing,' Meyer says. 'I don't know where it came from. I'm not a vampirey person.' She thinks she understands the appeal of them, though. She thinks people love them because 'they're beautiful, they're cultured, they can live for ever. Vampires have that alluring edge to their horror.' She later expanded on her thinking, explaining further the differences between vampires and other scary fictional creatures. 'My personal theory is that, more than other monsters, vampires fascinate humans because of their double nature,' she said. 'Not only do they frighten us but they also attract us. Most of the other monsters we like to scare ourselves with are traditionally ugly and repulsive – zombies, blobs, giant spiders – but vampires, on the other hand, have many attributes we envy: they are beautiful, they are eternally young, they are strong, they are intelligent and well spoken, they often dress better than we do and they sometimes even live in castles. The sophisticated vampire poses the question: Is it worth it to be evil if you can have everything you want?'

It was a sophisticated vampire that Stephenie was aiming to create in the story she was sitting down to write that day – not that she was writing with any form of definite plan. She was certainly not expecting to write what would form part of a bestselling novel. Instead, she just set down in words the basic framework and dialogue of what had come to her in her sleep. All the same, she *was* writing and, as many novelists have found, once you are doing that it can lead you anywhere. 'It was better than the dream, getting to make it real,' she said.

The process, the journey, itself can frequently be enjoyable. 'The dream is what started me off,' she recalled. 'I had fun that day. It was just ten pages. I didn't think about writing it as a book. I just wanted to see what happened next. I know when I started writing because I had it marked on my calendar.'

So there we have it: 2 June 2003 is the date on which the *Twilight* saga was born. What an enormously successful entity it was to prove to be! Its creator Stephenie quickly found that she wanted to write beyond the meadow scene. She became enchanted by her characters, who at this point were still merely 'he' and 'she', and wanted to broaden their experiences and their story. 'I was eager to know more about what would happen to these intriguing characters,' said Stephenie. 'So I kept typing, letting the story go where it wanted to go.'

She wrote on in the days that followed, and soon she was gathering momentum and motivation as the story took shape.

'From that point on, not one day passed that I did not write something,' she recalled. 'On bad days, I would only type out a page or two; on good days, I would finish a chapter and then some.' She could not, she added, stay away from her computer. She was drawn to her desk so she could continue to embellish the story of the duo, who would soon get names of their own.

First, she named the vampire. For him, she decided she would 'use a name that had once been considered romantic, but that had fallen out of popularity for decades' – Edward. It was a name that had been used for key characters in two of Stephenie's favourite novels. In Charlotte Brontë's *Jane Eyre*, Edward Rochester is a Byronic hero and the master of Thornfield Manor. In *Sense and Sensibility* by Jane Austen, Edward Ferrars is the elder of Fanny

Dashwood's two brothers. He is introduced in the novel in less than complimentary terms. 'He was not handsome, and his manners required intimacy to make them pleasing,' wrote Austen. (His character was played by leading English actor Hugh Grant in the 1995 film adaptation of the novel.)

These two characters were the ones that led her to decide what to call her male character. Beyond these there had been precious few iconic Edwards in cultural history. Edward Scissorhands was an uncommonly gentle eponymous leading character in a smash-hit film, and Edward the Blue Engine was a kind enough character in *Thomas the Tank Engine*. Neither had the literary icon status of Messrs Rochester and Ferrars, to say the least. Stephenie decided that it was time to bring the name Edward back into popularity and gave it to her handsome vampire character. His surname would be Cullen.

For the female character, she found it much harder to decide on the name. 'Nothing I named her seemed just right,' she said of her tribulations in making the decision. 'After spending so much time with her, I loved her like a daughter, and no name was good enough. Finally, inspired by that love, I gave her the name I was saving for my daughter, who had never shown up and was unlikely to put in an appearance at this point: Isabella. Huzzah!'

However, the character would become known more widely as Bella, the Italian word for beauty. Stephenie now had the names for her two lead characters: huzzah indeed! At this point, they were just characters in a story that Stephenie had yet even to tell anyone else she was writing. She loved them all the more for that, though. They were her secret friends, part of her little world that she could disappear into.

Which is exactly why the next thing she needed for the story was a location. Given certain key factors she had in mind for the story, there was one important detail she had to get right. 'I knew I needed someplace ridiculously rainy,' she wrote on her official website. 'I turned to Google, as I do for all my research needs, and looked for the place with the most rainfall in the US. This turned out to be the Olympic Peninsula in Washington State. I pulled up maps of the area and studied them, looking for something small, out of the way, surrounded by forest . . . And there, right where I wanted it to be, was a tiny town called "Forks." It couldn't have been more perfect if I had named it myself. I did a Google image search on the area, and if the name hadn't sold me, the gorgeous photographs would have done the trick.'

Forks was a strange name for a town – it's actually a city – and an even stranger name for a book. Yet it was that name that she initially chose to be the title of the story she was creating. Would it ever have gained its iconic status if that had remained the title of the book?

It was still a long way from turning into a complete, coherent story, though, let alone a full novel with blockbuster-movie potential. Still, Stephenie continued to write away managing to complete chapters at an alarmingly fast rate considering her other domestic responsibilities. She found the work to be 'an unusual experience because I felt obsessive about the process. It wasn't like me to be so focused[;] it's hard to be, with all the kids around.'

Indeed, she has compared the creative experience to that of a dam bursting, such was the rate at which she was able to write the story. She admits that, with so little time on her hands, she did lose a fair amount of sleep, as she often wrote in the early hours of the morning. Sometimes she would give in during those wee small hours and go to bed. However, then, as she lay there with her eyes closed, her mind would race, still alive with new ideas.

At other times she wrote with one of her children sitting on her. 'I did a lot of writing with my one-year-old on my lap,' she said. 'He's kind of a monkey, so he could cling and I would type around him.'

The more she wrote, the more the story took shape and it quickly became an obsession for her. While watching television or listening to music on the radio, she would watch and listen through the eyes and ears of her characters. When a song began, she would think which character from her story would like the song most, and which least. On television, she would wonder which of the actors in the scene could play which character in her novel.

Just as Edward would later speak to Bella in her head during the *New Moon* novel, so did he and Bella speak to the author. 'All this time, Bella and Edward were, quite literally, voices in my head,' she wrote on her website. 'They simply wouldn't shut up. I'd stay up as late as I could stand trying to get all the stuff in my mind typed out, and then crawl, exhausted, into bed (my baby still wasn't sleeping through the night, yet) only to have another conversation start in my head. I hated to lose anything by forgetting, so I'd get up and head back down to the computer.

'Eventually, I got a pen and notebook for beside my bed to jot notes down so I could get some freakin' sleep. It was always an exciting challenge in the morning to try to decipher the stuff I'd scrawled across the page in the dark.'

It was worth the effort, though, to decipher those bleary-eyed, darkness-surrounded notes. (She keeps a notebook by her bed to this day.) Every little helped as she put together the different ideas and inspirations in a coherent whole that was becoming a magnificent piece of work. Writing was really working for Stephenie.

Indeed, she felt that with this process she was connecting with a skill that had been hidden previously, but was now soaring to the surface in glorious fashion. 'I started out just so I wouldn't forget the story, but I kept going. I really felt like it was a situation where I had a talent I was not using; I had buried it. And that was my kick-start. I was supposed to be doing something with this talent.'

It was as if she were ready to turn into a butterfly, having sheltered in the larval stage previously. How she would soar with her newfound wings! But her new life was not to be without its sacrifices.

'Being a mother is about the most full-time job you could have,' she says. 'And I had three little boys, so there was no time to do something else. But I was obsessed with the story from the first day. I'd painted before and I'd done a couple of other little creative endeavours because it felt good to be creative, but they weren't completely fulfilling.'

With writing, though, she felt completely fulfilled. 'It was like I had just found my favourite flavour of ice cream,' she said. 'All of a sudden, there it is: "This is what I should have been doing for the last thirty years. What was I thinking?" So I just kept going with it.'

Keeping going, finding the time around her domestic duties, meant that other things had to go out of the window for Stephenie. Chief among these was contact with the outside world beyond her family and the walls of their home. She dropped out of her scrapbook club, stopped seeing friends and put an end to her trips to the local cinema. She became a mysterious person, dropping out of any unnecessary distractions altogether. 'I became somewhat of a hermit that summer,' she says.

Her secretiveness over what she was writing was

complete and all-encompassing – she had not even told Pancho at first what was under way. Theirs was not a marriage that was full of secrets, but for now she wanted to keep what she was writing private. Somehow, she felt, she would write better if she was not sharing the details with others at this point, a sentiment she still lives by.

'So he was mystified,' she says. 'And a little irritated that I was hogging the computer all the time.'

Nor was she thinking even remotely about publishing or commercial details. It was her story, and for now it was staying that way. 'I was really protective and shy about it because it's a vampire romance,' she said. 'It's still embarrassing to say those words – it sounds so cheesy. It's not like I was going to tell him that I was writing this story about vampires, because he was just going to be even more perturbed.'

This, quite naturally, made for a slightly tense atmosphere in the house. 'We're not either of us very docile people,' she admits. 'We argue all the time because that's our personalities. We didn't get in mean arguments, but I'm sure we argued over it because we argue about everything – we argue about milk.'

Her elder sister Emily was one of the first people to notice that Stephenie had gone quiet, and also the quickest to start investigating what was going on. She thus became the first person to whom Stephenie admitted what she was up to. 'It was abnormal that she wasn't talking to me,' recalled Emily. 'I called her and said, "What's going on? Why aren't you calling me any more?"'

Stephenie felt for a variety of reasons that it was time to come clean to somebody about the exciting project she was working on. 'I don't keep secrets from Emily,' she says. 'I thought she'd laugh, but it turns out she's a big *Buffy* fan, which I didn't know. She wanted to see it, and, on the one hand, I was very shy about it, but, on the other hand, I was in love with it, so I wanted her to see it.'

So she told Emily what she was doing and began to email her the chapters as she finished writing them. Her sister was impressed with what she was reading. This admiration was not the result of sibling loyalty or politeness. She was genuinely becoming hooked on the unfolding story. 'I would call and hound her, and I was always there bugging her,' she says. 'I've read *Twilight* I don't know how many times.'

The book had its first confirmed fan, and it was Emily who sought to persuade Stephenie to try to publish the story. It was then time to tell Pancho what she had been up to all the time she'd spent hogging the family computer. It was not an easy process to break the news to him. 'I had as hard a time telling him I was writing a story about vampires as Edward did telling Bella he was one,' she says, smiling. It must have been a very strange conversation to say the least.

With the story finished, Stephenie could begin to consider taking her sister's urging seriously. First, though, she was struck by another slumbertime fantasy. 'I actually did have a dream after *Twilight* was finished, of Edward coming to visit me,' said Stephenie. 'Only I had gotten it wrong and he did drink blood like every other vampire and you couldn't live on animals the way I'd written it. We had this conversation and he was terrifying.'

The story had been inspired by a dream, and another dream had formed the dark coda to the completion of its creation. Stephenie was still not, initially at least, considering it to be a professional venture. Instead, it was just about her own fun. 'I didn't think about publishing at all until it was entirely done – I was just telling myself a story. Writing just for the sake of writing, just for my own pleasure.'

That was about to change, however, as she gave full consideration to her sister's encouragement. Could it be that Emily was not merely being a kind, polite family member when she said she was convinced it could be a commercial success? Indeed, whisper it quietly, but could it be true that she had on her hands a genuine masterpiece with bestselling potential?

The only way to find out was to submit the story to the scrutiny of the publishing industry and see if they liked it. However, she was very unaware of how to go about doing this. 'Movies lie to us!' she joked when outlining the differences between how the big screen portrays the publishing process and the harsh reality. She jokes that anyone who learns how 'insanely impossible' the process is will never be able to enjoy the film *Cheaper by the Dozen*, which includes an aspiring author called Kate. Stephenie was about to get a crash course in the realities of the process.

'To put it mildly, I was naïve about publishing,' she said. 'I thought it worked like this: you printed a copy of your novel, wrapped it up in brown paper, and sent it off to a publishing house.' She laughs when looking back at her naïveté. She used Google and learned more about how to try to get a book published. She found it upsetting and almost offputting. 'The whole setup with query letters, literary agents, simultaneous submissions versus exclusive submissions, synopses et cetera was extremely intimidating, and I almost quit there.'

However, she felt so strongly about Edward and Bella as characters that she found the motivation via them to carry on. She felt compelled to bring them to the wider world's attention. 'It certainly wasn't belief in my fabulous talent that made me push forward: I think it was just that I loved my characters so much, and they were so real to me, that I wanted other people to know them, too.'

Stephenie found the process genuinely scary, and when she recalls those days she has physical reactions. One of the early websites she studied was WritersMarket.com. *Writer's Market* was originally just a book, but a mightily influential one. First published back in 1921, it quickly built a reputation for itself as the definitive printed guide to getting published. Authors – established, aspiring and merely dreaming – leaf through the pages of the annual guide with its peerless combination of contact details for agents and publishers, tips and other invaluable resources. With the dawn of the Internet, an online version was built, which Stephenie perused, and she used her credit card to subscribe to the full version of the site, which gave her access to a mine of information and tips, as well as the option of a regular email with tips and tricks.

'It was something like three bucks a month,' she remembers. Although the service was extremely helpful, it was also intimidating for Stephenie. 'When I started looking into publishing on the Internet, it seemed so complicated – writing queries and all that,' she said. 'I'm kind of surprised that I didn't quit at that point. That is normally what I would do: give up on things that frighten me.' She kept going, though, after finding something steely inside herself.

Another online resource that she used was suggested to her by her little sister Heidi. It was the homepage of author Janet Evanovich, who writes powerfully on the site about her own experiences on the road to getting published, including collecting rejection letters in a huge cardboard box. 'She said if you want to be a writer as a profession, then treat it like a job. Put in the hours. Set aside time for writing, and then make yourself sit down and do it. Sometimes it's easy – the words flow and you can get a lot done. Other times it's hard, and you might only get one sentence done in an hour. But that's better than nothing.'

Stephenie read all the pages on the website, including the Q&A. There, Evanovich mentioned the agency Writers House. She described it reverentially as 'the real thing'. Therefore, when it came to compiling her own shortlist of agents to approach with her story, Stephenie put Writers House at the top of the list. She considered it 'the most desirable [but] least likely' option.

So, with her shortlist complete, she was ready to send out a single-page synopsis of the story together with a covering letter. She says she still feels 'residual butterflies in my stomach' when she drives past the post box she pushed the envelopes into. 'I sent letters out to fifteen [agents] and I got, I think, nine rejections and five "no answers". I only got one bite, but it was from the "dream on, Stephenie" agency at the top of my list.' From, in other words, that most desirable but least likely prospect – Writers House.

A famous literary agency on West 21st Street in Manhattan, it was formed in 1973, the year Stephenie was born. Al Zuckerman, a novelist and playwright, was one of the founding members and it went on to become a prestigious respected agency that combined fine commercial clout with creative know-how. As such, it represented a dream firm for many authors, aspiring and otherwise. The offices it occupies were built by William Waldorf and John Jacob Astor III in

1881. Stephenie will have been wowed by the façade of the building, which is Victorian in style and has fine red bricks combined with polished granite and fine terracotta. The agency's meeting room is a fine, antique-panelled affair that oozes success and – in all senses of the word – wealth. It would be hard to attend a meeting there and not believe that one had already arrived in the world of publishing.

When Stephenie's envelope arrived at the office, it was put on to what is known as the 'slush pile'. This is an accurately dismissive term for the pile of unsolicited mail that exists in the office of all agencies (and all publishers). It might include entire manuscripts, synopses, pitching letters and probably a few bribes here and there. Most of the mail in such a pile will go unread. However, occasionally a member of staff – normally a junior one – will be sent to leaf through as much of what lies there as he or she can stand, on the off-chance of discovering a hidden gem. There they will be greeted by a lot of material that is simply unpublishable. From hellish poetry, to thinly veiled autobiographical novels, to books that amount to little more than an account of what the author did on his or her holidays. The staff member sifting through this will need enormous patience, and the ability to speed-read would be a major advantage, too, because some of the above examples are among the more sensible foundations for a book. An author writing in the *Guardian* newspaper gave a few examples she had read while sifting through a slush pile in a publisher's office in her first post-university job.

'I won an award in my reception class for writing,' opened one covering letter, 'and ever since then I have known that it is my destiny to be a writer. I enclose the first 600 pages of my fantasy space opera.' Another took a more bawdy turn. 'We are a normal Leicestershire couple, until the lights go down,' began the synopsis. 'This is the true story of our erotic journey, illustrated with woodcuts.' Then there were the straightforwardly bizarre. 'I am a 35-year-old mother of four children and two dogs and I have an unfortunate foot rash. I have written a novel about a 35-year-old mother of four children and two dogs who has an unfortunate foot rash.'

She recalls that it was novels aimed at young people that often veered furthest from being publishable. She could afford to give all such contributions only the most cursory of assessments, and then she would send out the standard rejection letter time after time, after signing it as illegibly as she could, for fear of an angry phone call from the rejected author, which often came within moments of the arrival of the letter.

Working at Writers House when Stephenie's unsolicited submission arrived was a young assistant called Genevieve, or Gen to those who know her better. She was going through the pile of mail when she happened upon Stephenie's synopsis. She was impressed by it and asked Stephenie to send in the first three chapters for her consideration.

'I didn't find out until much later just how lucky I was,' said Stephenie. 'It turns out that Gen didn't know that 130,000 words is a whole heck of a lot of words. If she'd known that 130K words would equal 500 pages, she probably wouldn't have asked to see it. But she didn't know (picture me wiping the sweat from my brow), and she did ask for the first three chapters.'

Stephenie was 'thrilled' to have got a promising reply from what was her dream, best-case-scenario agency. However, she was also a touch concerned because she did not believe the opening chapters of the book to be the strongest part. All the same, she did exactly as asked and mailed the chapters off. Then she did something familiar to many aspiring authors – she waited.

Not for long, though. The next communication came from Writers House just a few weeks later – which was a fast response in such a situation. When their letter dropped through Stephenie's letterbox that morning, she was beside herself with nerves. 'I could barely get it open, my hands were so weak with fear,' she said. She need not have worried, because, as she soon realised, 'it was a very nice letter'.

The typed letter explained that Gen had loved the chapters, and had even gone to the trouble of underlining that clause in pen – twice. She then asked Stephenie to send the entire manuscript. 'That was the exact moment when I realised that I might actually see *Twilight* in print, and really one of the happiest points in my whole life,' says Stephenie. 'I did a lot of screaming.' She still has the letter to this day.

When the full manuscript arrived, Gen passed it to a senior agent at Writers House. Her name was Jodi Reamer. The agent was quickly blown away by what she read. Reamer had been with the agency for around eight years when Stephenie's story came her way and she had spent those years 'handling just about every type of fiction and nonfiction, adult and children's book project imaginable'. Reamer, impressed with the story, decided she wanted to 'represent' the book and rang Stephenie to tell her the good news.

It was a very, very exciting phone call for the stay-at-home mum. 'I tried really hard to sound like a professional and a grownup during that conversation, but I'm not sure if I fooled her.'

It didn't matter, because Reamer was as keen on Stephenie as Stephenie was on Reamer. She describes Reamer as 'the über-agent. I couldn't have ended up in better hands. She's part lawyer, part ninja . . . and a pretty amazing editor in her own right.' The two became good friends, too, during the process towards publication.

The first part of that process was a fortnight in which author and agent worked on polishing up the story to as close to perfection as they could manage. This included dropping Stephenie's original name for the book – *Forks* – and coming up with a new one, as we shall see.

'Then we polished up a few rough spots, and Jodi sent it out to nine different publishing houses,' says Stephenie. 'This really messed with my ability to sleep, but luckily I wasn't in suspense for long.'

Among the publishing-house editors who received the book was Megan Tinley, the editor at the Little, Brown imprint. She read the manuscript while on a cross-country plane journey during Thanksgiving weekend. She was so excited as she sat there, leafing through the pages, that she could not wait for the plane to land so she could contact Reamer and do the deal to sign the book.

'It was the combination of desire and danger that drew me in,' she recalls of her first reading of the manuscript, sitting thousands of feet in the air. 'I could not put it down.' She read on, and by the time she reached the middle of the story she was already convinced that, if her publisher could sign the book, they would have a big hit. 'On a gut level, I knew I had a bestseller on my hands when I was halfway through the manuscript.'

No wonder she was keen to get on the phone to Reamer and negotiate a deal. However, the negotiation was not to be quite as smooth as she hoped. Tinley offered to pay $300,000 for a three-book deal, starting with the story. For an unknown, previously unpublished author to be offered $100,000 per book was amazing. Meyer was overjoyed when she learned that this was what a major publishing house was offering her. The figure she had been hoping for was $10,000. She was going to use the money to pay off the minivan she had on hire purchase.

So, when she learned she was being offered 30 times that sum, she was stunned by the news. It would have been beyond her wildest dreams. 'I honestly thought Jodi was pulling my leg,' she said.

Imagine her surprise, then, when Reamer told her that she had turned down the offer and demanded a higher sum. To be precise, Reamer had asked for a whopping $1,000,000 for the deal. Stephenie tried to play it cool, but she was stunned and almost sickened with shock at the sums that were being discussed for her work.

'It was the most surreal day,' she says. 'I almost threw up. Eli was with me, so he was thinking, Mommy lost her mind for a little while,' she says of her youngest child, then a year old. 'I was on the phone with Jodi trying to be all professional. "Yes, I'd love that. That's great." And then I called my sister and I could hardly talk. Eli was following me around on his play phone going, "Ha-ha-ha-ha-ha," imitating me.'

She waited by the phone to find out the outcome of the negotiations. She might, quite reasonably, have feared at times that Reamer's hardball tactics might end with the negotiations breaking down entirely.

Stephenie was learning fast. Only months before, she

had been entirely unaware of the ways and politics of the publishing industry. Now she was suddenly the subject of a fierce back-and-forth between a leading agency and a top publishing house. These were heady times for the stay-at-home mum, who was finding it very hard to believe the level of interest that was being expressed in her book. Indeed, she plummeted into moods of intense paranoia, in which she imagined a rather fanciful scenario was at work. She said, 'For a very long time, I was convinced it was a really cruel practical joke, but I couldn't imagine who would go to these wild extremes to play a hoax on such an insignificant little *hausfrau*.'

Soon, publisher Megan Tingley picked up the phone and responded to Reamer's counter-offer. She would not go all the way to the million-dollar sum that Reamer had asked for. Instead, she offered to meet the agent at $750,000. This was comfortably more than double the initial offer and was also the largest sum that the publisher had ever given to an unpublished, unknown author. Stephenie was already making publishing history, before a single book of hers had even been printed. The reader can only imagine the reaction of the nervous Stephenie as she picked up the phone, put it to her ear and learned of the deal that her agent had struck for her.

She and Reamer accepted the offer and the deal was done. But, despite their newfound riches, the Meyer couple did not change. 'My big splurge was letting my husband quit his job and go back to school full time,' says Stephenie. 'The other was when we bought an Infiniti G35 coupé with the spoiler and all the extras. I love that car!' To put the figure in some perspective, JK Rowling received a mere £1,500 advance for the first *Harry Potter* book.

Reamer had done her client proud. The agent was no fan of vampire stories, but she had been confident that she had a hit on her hands throughout the negotiation with Little, Brown.

Tingley said, 'I know I'm on to something big when I respond to something that is outside my favourite genres. I'm not a vampire fan. And I'm not a romance fan, either. But this book has vampires, romance and suspense. Also, the heroine is appealing because she's every girl. She's not rich, she's not gorgeous, but she's strong.'

Stephenie, though, was rich indeed as a result of the deal Reamer struck for her. 'I wish I would have believed in myself and started writing sooner.'

Little wonder. However much at heart she remained something of an 'everywoman', Stephenie was now richer to the tune of three-quarters of a million dollars. Just six months earlier she had sat down and written the details of the meadow-scene dream she'd had that June evening. How far she had come, and so quickly!

'It's been a real whirlwind – more like a lightning strike,' she said.

Would-be authors across the world struggle year

after year to even gain the attention of a publisher or agent, but Stephenie had shot straight to the finishing line in half a year. She said she was aware of her good fortune, and would later admit to feeling some guilt over her success. During an interview shortly after the publication of *Twilight*, she reflected, 'Ohhh, other writers are going to hate me.'

It was not merely fortune, though, and there was no need for her to feel any guilt whatsoever. Hers was already becoming a story that anyone with a heart could only be delighted to become aware of. An ordinary mum who becomes the subject of a publishing battle is the stuff that dreams are made of. The fact that the story concerned was the result of a dream made it even more fantastic. The advance she received for *Twilight* would soon seem peanuts when set against her impending multimillionaire status. But first there was a lot of work to do.

The publishers, Little, Brown, were happy that they had a hit on their hands, but were slightly wary of Meyer, about whom they knew next to nothing. They duly sent an employee – a member of the company's publicity team – to Arizona to meet Stephenie. The author laughs that she felt as if she were being vetted. They wanted, she suspects, to check that she 'wasn't wearing a skirt over my jeans or something'. The publishers and Stephenie also discussed changes to be made to the manuscript. For a start, as we've seen, they wanted her to change the title. 'We played around with a lot of different titles, and nothing seemed to convey the right feel. We brainstormed through emails for about a week. The word *twilight* was on a list of "words with atmosphere" that I sent her. Though these words were meant to be used in combination with something else, the word *twilight* stood out to both of us.'

So it was that the novel was renamed *Twilight*. With the benefit of hindsight, it seems remarkable that it was ever close to being called *Forks*, which is a remarkably unevocative title to say the least. Stephenie, though, admits to still having a 'soft spot' for her original title. She has also published on her personal website some rough images she had knocked up for the cover of the book, back in the days before it had been signed up by a publisher.

There were also changes to be made to the story itself. Chief among these was a reworking of the ending. Stephenie had not written the story with the intention of making it into a series. Therefore, the story came to a very definite conclusion in her first version, one that would not allow so easily for there to be sequels. So she reworked the ending to leave the story open for it to become a series. There were other, small changes to be made. For instance, for the prom scene, Stephenie had Bella being driven to the event in an Aston Martin V12 Vanquish car. The decision was made for her to be transported in a more modest vehicle. Stephenie filed away the Vanquish for use in a future novel.

She had to learn to toughen up as a person during this process, as her cherished creation was forced to undergo alterations in the face of the cold reality of commercial publishing. 'Editing is a lot more invasive than I thought it was,' Stephenie said. 'Very emotional and hurtful . . . it's hard to develop that thick skin to handle the critique.' Hard indeed, because, as she admits, she was at first 'pretty intimidated by the editors and the publishers', adding that she felt like a schoolgirl being told what to do by the headteacher. However, she did her best to hold her own when it came to changes in the characters. 'When they said, "This is how we would like this to go," I was like, "Edward would never do that! That's impossible!"'

She adds, 'If it was something [threatening] the characters, I could hold my own. And that taught me the confidence I needed to continue with a career in writing.'

Further revisions and improvements were made until Stephenie was prepared to surrender the book to be copy-edited. She was then presented with proofs. This would be the final time that she would get to make changes to the text before the book was sent out to the printers. How to bring closure to such a personal, creative process? Stephenie would later admit that she never reaches a point in each book's publishing journey at which she believes she has finished with the work and that it has reached its perfect state, allowing her to walk away from it entirely satisfied. 'I do want to make one point about writing,' she would tell students at the

Arizona State University in 2005. 'Even today, if I turned to any page in the story, I could probably find at least five words I would want to change. So you never really finish. You just find a good place in the process to quit.'

Having quit, she relaxed as the book was printed. This was easy to do, because she was entirely unaware of what was ahead for her when the book was published. Her hopes at this point were modest by any standards, let alone those of an author who was about to become an international bestselling sensation.

'My expectation was that, maybe, if I'm really lucky, one of my books would get to a shelf in a bookstore somewhere,' she said. 'That would have been enough for me.'

True, she could never have known what a fuss was about to be made of her work. But, even then, it must be said that these were very low-key expectations.

However, her expectations were to be given an enormous boost when she heard that not only did she have a book deal but work was afoot to create a feature film of her novel. At the start of 2004, the music channel MTV and film production company Maverick Films, which was founded by Madonna and Guy Oseary in 2001, joined forces and negotiated for the rights to make a screenplay of *Twilight*. It was to be the first joint venture undertaken by MTV and Maverick. The plan was to release the film via MTV's Viacom sister company Paramount Pictures. This was enormously exciting for Stephenie. Before her novel even hit the shelves, she had been approached for the rights to a film version of the book. Given her love of rock music, the planned involvement of MTV would have thrilled her all the more. As we shall see, the route to the big screen was not an entirely straightforward one for *Twilight*. However, for now, she sat basking in the glory of having a lucrative three-book deal and had also sold the film rights to the first book.

So what was the story contained within the pages of *Twilight*? Stephenie summarises it succinctly. 'It's mostly about a vampire who falls in love with a normal human girl,' she says. 'And sort of the inherent problems with dating vampires.'

The story begins with Isabella (Bella) Swan moving from Phoenix, Arizona, to Forks in Washington to stay with her father. Although nervous, she proves popular at the school and soon attracts the attention of a strange family called the Cullens. She is mesmerised by one of them in particular – Edward. His brooding good looks and mysterious character fascinate her. He displays supernatural powers, such as when he saves her from being run down in the school car park. As her intrigue builds, she concludes – following an illuminating chat with a family friend called Jacob – that Edward and his family are vampires. However, Bella and Edward are fast falling in love, and nothing is about to stop that. Soon, their relationship is attracting the attention of another vampire clan, one of whom vows to kill Bella. A grandstand conclusion sees her nearly killed by the hostile vampire, saved by Edward. He takes her to the school prom, where she sets up the premise of the sequels by announcing her desire to become a vampire herself.

At the heart of the story's appeal is the dilemma that Edward and Bella face due to his vampire status: he loves Bella in the normal ways but the scent of her blood is desirable to him as a vampire. 'Well that's what gives you the tension,' says Stephenie. 'It's that extra aspect where it's not just life or death because my heart's going to be broken. It's life or death as in you could die in the next fifteen minutes. I tend to be drawn towards fiction with fantasy elements just because you can take normal humans and sort of push them beyond what we really have to deal with every day. And so, to have people who are by definition monsters who don't want to be monsters, and the conflict in that, it makes for some really interesting stuff to work with.'

Interesting indeed. In full, it proved a gripping, strangely hypnotic story. A strangely old-fashioned one as well. Given her unconventional upbringing, under the rules of the Mormon faith and the strict ways of her university, it would be surprising if all these experiences had not influenced her work. Throughout the story, the characters are showing great restraint. Edward does not bite Bella, and the rest of the Cullen family constantly struggle with their vampire urges. Rather than kill humans, they search for animals to satisfy their bloodlust. Edward and Bella do not give in to their sexual urges, either. Nowadays, young-adult novels often stray into far racier territory than Stephenie allows with her work. This is due to the influence of her religion. 'Mormon themes do come through in *Twilight*,' she agrees. 'Free agency – I see that in the Cullens. The vampires made this choice to be something more – that's my belief, the importance of free will to be human.'

As to her inspiration for the characters, Stephenie is insistent about where they came from. 'Edward is too perfect to exist in reality,' she said. 'I've known pieces of Jacob in various forms – he's much more likely to occur in nature. Much more human and much more possible.'

Her inspiration for characters came from many places, including her beloved *X-Men* cartoons. 'I think that really came into play when I was subconsciously forming the Cullen family,' she says of the *X-Men* link. 'Though I certainly wasn't thinking about Cyclops when I was writing about them, I think it was there in the layers underneath.' She included lots of legends of the Quileute tribe – who are a Native American people. She drew on true stories for this. 'All of the legends in the books are part of their tradition, the werewolves and so on,' she says. 'The only legend that is not part of the Quileute tradition is the part I devised specifically to fit the Cullens.'

Fascination – and on the Internet feverish discussion

– surrounds so many aspects of the book. Having named the book *Twilight* – after it was temporarily christened *Forks* – Stephenie opened up debate as to why she chose such a title. For the foreign editions, though, it was often given entirely new titles. In Finland it was called *Temptation*, in France *Fascination* and Germany *Until Dawn*. 'It isn't absolutely perfect; to be honest, I don't think there is a perfect title for this book (or if there is, I've never heard it),' she wrote on her personal website. However, *Twilight* is not just an evocative title: it is also a highly fitting one for the story and its themes. The word can, after all, refer to two separate times of day: the early evening and the early morning. It is a time that is neither dark nor light. The word is all about ambiguity – a key theme of the book. Even good (light) and evil (dark) are interchangeable in Stephenie's story. '[It is] both a time of day as well as "being in the twilight of one's life", which, in a sense Bella is,' said publisher Megan Tingley.

As well as altering the title, the foreign editions also made other changes to the book. For instance, in Japan they divided the book into three smaller volumes. The first one was called 'The Boy Whom I Love is a Vampire', the second was 'Blood Tastes Sadness' and the third 'The Vampire Family in the Darkness'. In Denmark they broke the story into two, so the book could easily fit through customers' letterboxes. The same fate had befallen the *Harry Potter* series in the Scandinavian country.

The cover of *Twilight* is striking and iconic. Against a plain black background are two hands, holding a red apple. The two arms are forming a 'V' shape, suggestive of the word vampire to the observant reader. The apple is ripe, crisp and perfectly formed. 'The apple on the cover of *Twilight* represents "forbidden fruit",' explained Stephenie. 'I used the scripture from Genesis . . . because I loved the phrase "the fruit of the knowledge of good and evil." Isn't this exactly what Bella ends up with? A working knowledge of what good is, and what evil is. The nice thing about the apple is it has so many symbolic roots.'

Among the symbolic roots that Stephenie has enjoyed is the apple that the Queen makes in the Snow White story. In disguise, the Queen offers it to Snow White, who on eating it sinks into a coma. 'One bite and you're frozen for ever in a state of not-quite death,' marvels Stephenie. She also enjoyed the stories of the Golden Apple, which appears in numerous folk stories, most notably Greek mythology. In this genre the apple is often the force that sparks lust and trouble. 'Apples are quite the versatile fruit,' she wrote. 'In the end, I love the beautiful simplicity of the [front cover] picture. To me it says: choice.'

For some of the foreign editions, though, as well as choice they also wanted a bit of gore. For instance, the Spanish publisher told Tingley, 'I love your cover, and I'd love to frame that as a beautiful piece of art. But, for our audience, [the cover] has to have blood on it. It has to be obvious.'

An amusing irony: in the wake of her tying up the deal with Little, Brown, as Stephenie basked in the glory of her contract, she encountered a touch of the response that other authors are more familiar with – the stinging rejection. 'Be brave, even when you get rejections,' she advises budding authors who pay a visit to her personal website. 'All bestselling authors got rejections.'

Indeed, they do – even Stephenie. She received a harshly phrased rejection from an editor at another publisher, who was unaware when penning the rejection that Stephenie had just secured the Little, Brown deal. 'The meanest rejection I got came after Little, Brown had picked me up for a three-book deal, so it didn't bother me at all,' she recalls. 'I'll admit that I considered sending back a copy of that rejection stapled to the write-up my deal got in *Publisher's Weekly*, but I took the higher road.'

A higher road that included the start of her work on the sequel to *Twilight*. This happened straight after her finishing with the opening novel of what was to become a saga – and happened quite naturally for Stephenie. 'I found myself writing multiple epilogues – hundred-plus-page epilogues,' she says. 'I quickly realised I wasn't ready to stop writing about Bella and Edward.' Which was just as well, because, as she was about to discover, the reading public was nowhere near being ready to stop reading about them.

Twilight was published in the autumn of 2005. The initial print run was for 75,000 copies (to give this figure some context, the first *Harry Potter* book had a print run of just 1,000 – half of which were distributed to libraries). Within the industry, there was quite a buzz about the book. This unknown, debut author had received such a big advance for the title that there was a fascination over the whole business. The book-trade journal *Publishers' Weekly* led the charge of admiration, with a glowing review of the book.

'The main draw here is Bella's infatuation with outsider Edward,' it said, 'the sense of danger inherent in their love, and Edward's inner struggle – a perfect metaphor for the sexual tension that accompanies adolescence. These will be familiar to nearly every teen, and will keep readers madly flipping the pages of Meyer's tantalizing debut.' This was a positive verdict for the book, and very much pleased Stephenie as she sat and waited for the wider media to deliver their own verdicts on her debut novel.

Nowadays, with her stature so enormous, any book published by Stephenie is guaranteed widespread critical scrutiny. However, when *Twilight* hit the shelves, there was no way of knowing whether anyone would review the book, let alone what they would write. One of the first journals to follow *Publishers' Weekly* was the *School Library Journal*. 'Meyer adds an eerie new twist to mismatched, star-crossed lovers theme: predator falls for prey, human falls for vampire,' wrote the publication's reviewer. 'The novel's danger-factor skyrockets as the excitement of secret love and hushed affection morphs into a terrifying race to stay alive. Realistic, subtle, succinct and easy to follow, *Twilight* will have readers dying to sink their teeth into it.'

Soon it was chosen as a *New York Times* Editor's Choice and a *Publishers' Weekly* Best Book of the Year, while *Teen People* put it on their Hot List. The book was very swiftly receiving thumbs-ups in some important places. Could there be a *real* groundswell of excitement building up for Stephenie's debut work?

There surely could, because, when the regional media in the USA delivered their verdicts to their readers, they were full of positivity. Karyn Saemann of the *Capital Times* wrote, '*Twilight* is a well-written, engrossing young adult spin on the classic vampire stories of old . . . With occasional, minor exceptions where the writing is bogged down by mythical vampire background, this is a quick-paced, thrilling and fun read that has at its core an unexpectedly tender love story. It's an excellent first try for Meyer, and I hope not her last.'

Mary Harris Russell of the *Chicago Tribune* was ready to have her say, too. 'Imagine you're stuck attending high school in a foggy village on Washington state's Olympic Peninsula, with your mostly non-custodial parent, who just happens to be the police chief,' she began, before delivering the twist in the tale that would appeal to her readers. 'There's not much sunshine for this former Phoenix girl, Isabella Swan, but there is the most amazingly gorgeous boy, her new biology lab partner. Oh, did I mention he's a vampire? This vamp, however, is different, because he's part of a small pack trying to live a different way. Just how it all works out I won't say, but you should know that this vampire understands the importance of going to the prom. Who could ask for anything more?'

Who indeed. Clay McNear of the *Phoenix New Times*' verdict was of special interest to Stephenie, living as she did in the newspaper's catchment area. He praised it as: 'A dandy little thriller about vampirism and young love – Meyer's breezily seductive book, aimed at the young-adult market, is about a woman who's played for a sucker by a mysterious, toothy guy. Think *Dark Shadows*, only lighter.' (*Dark Shadows* is a Gothic soap opera that appeared on the ABC television network in the 1960s and 1970s, long before most of the *Twilight* fanbase were even born.)

What would Merri Lingdren make of Stephenie's work in her review for the *Wisconsin State Journal*? 'It begins like any good romance: New girl in town meets handsome boy and the chemistry between them sizzles,' she wrote, employing the already familiar 'delay' tactic of those reviewing the book, in which they delayed revealing the vampire element of the story for dramatic effect. 'As it turns out, that's all that Isabella and Edward's story shares with a conventional

90

high-school saga . . . Edward and Bella's intense physical attraction to one another skilfully demonstrates how less can be more, as the author evokes powerfully sensual scenes, while refraining from explicit physical descriptions.'

Here, the primness of Stephenie's storytelling was being picked up on and received positively. This would have been the source of some relief for Stephenie, who wanted to stay true to her faith and principles in writing this teenage story. In putting together a story about vampires she was already risking alienating herself from the LDS, so she was pleased to get a seal of approval critically for her lack of raciness in the novel. Not that the reviewers were unaware of the punch that was inherent in the story. As the *Detroit Free Press* said, 'Call this one a love story with real bite.'

Given its weightiness physically, there were concerns that younger readers would not be excited by the prospect of such a long read. Young people, went the theory, have a short attention span and are unlikely to become interested in big numbers in a book that will take up lots of their time. In this computer-game, Internet, text-message era, the youth were simply not geared up for books that would require a lot of their time and attention. There was justification for this point of view. In the digital, computer age, children's attention spans are different from those of their equivalents in the days when books were one of the main diversions that youngsters had on offer. Kellye Carter Crocker in the *Des Moines Register* had no time for these concerns. 'Don't be put off by the book's thick size; this first novel is a delectable quick read.'

Cindy Dach, marketing director at Changing Hands Bookstore in Tempe, Arizona, was also convinced that the novel's length – over 500 pages in some editions – would not deter readers, using solid evidence and reasoning. 'After *Harry Potter*, kids aren't afraid of big books,' she said. The logic was clear.

On and on came the praise. Stephenie is a modest, grounded person who considers herself a mother first and foremost. She will have needed to draw on all her powers of modesty to avoid getting carried away as people lined up to praise her.

Norah Piehl, writing on TeenReads.com, concluded of *Twilight*, 'Stephenie Meyer certainly leaves her own imprint on the genre. Her vampires are mysterious and alluring, with powers that alternately confirm and contradict traditional vampire lore. Bella's romantic dilemmas, klutziness, and loving relationships with her parents give her character depth and keep the narrative from becoming too dark. Although the novel is long, its pacing is steady and compelling until the end . . . *Twilight* is a gripping blend of romance and horror that will entice fans of both genres.'

Ilene Cooper of *Booklist* concluded of Stephenie's leading characters that: 'Their love is palpable, heightened by their touches, and teens will respond viscerally. There are some flaws here – a plot that could have been tightened, an overreliance on adjectives and adverbs to bolster dialogue – but this dark romance seeps into the soul. In the tradition of Anne Rice . . . this dark romance is gripping.'

So was it a vampire tale or a romance? As the book hit the shelves, one of the big questions had been exactly which shelves Stephenie's novel belonged on. Barnes & Noble placed it on their Horror shelves, while Borders initially planned to place it in Adult Romance. (Could Stephenie have later on been subtly alluding to this confusion when she wrote in *New Moon* about Bella's plane journey from America to Italy, when she says she could not tell whether the in-flight movie was supposed to be a horror or a romance?) Whichever shelves it was placed on, it was flying off them in spectacular numbers and was soon putting down roots in the bestseller lists of America. Stephenie had a hit on her hands Stateside.

There was just as much excitement and approval in Britain. One of the UK's oldest newspapers, *The Times*, kicked off the love-fest when it wrote that *Twilight* captured 'perfectly the teenage feeling of sexual tension and alienation'. Its rival, the *Daily Telegraph*, was also glowing, with an approving tone over the measured way Stephenie dealt with gory scenes. 'Not that you get to see much of the messy stuff,' wrote Christopher Middleton. 'With exemplary deftness, Meyer keeps any gory goings-on in the reader's imagination, rather than on the page. In the same way, the relationship between Bella and Edward is full of suppressed longing, but very little touching. All of which makes for a book that is exciting, but never explicit, thereby keeping it just about suitable for preteens.'

The 'Reading Notes' for the *Daily Telegraph* Book Club were more measured in their assessments, though. The writer commented on the lack of parental appearances. 'We're always commenting on it, but every children's book seems to get rid of the parents early on,' read the notes. 'Here, Bella is leaving her mother behind and going off to stay with a dad who lives on his own, is always out at work, and is the next best thing to an absent parent, in that he's a hands-off parent (apart from conveniently giving her a car as soon as she arrives). Even though he's the local chief of police, he doesn't seem to get involved with any of the action in the book (you might have thought the activities of bloodsucking vampires on his territory would have come to his attention!).'

There were also somewhat harsh words from 13-year-old Rebecca Clephan of Perth, Scotland. She was asked to review the book for the *Sunday Herald*. '*Twilight* is a very ordinary book, about an ordinary person and it has an ordinary beginning, middle and ending,' she wrote. 'It's the type of book that gets 100-per cent from English teachers but only 30-per cent from a teenage reader.' Damning words (and, incidentally, words that suggest that young Ms

Clephan – for all her pessimistic verdict – has a tongue sharp enough to make a career as a critic later in life). She concluded, 'I kept waiting for something to happen and this is not a good sign. I simply did not enjoy this book.'

There were to be harsher words, though. Perhaps the *Guardian*'s Bidisha (a single-named writer) was the most damning. 'The success . . . is puzzling because it's the most conservative example of an established young adult fantasy milieu of vampire subcultures and teen wolves. The genre's bestsellers usually come about because they flout outdated social norms, not reinforce them the way *Twilight* does.'

Despite the prediction that *Twilight* was a book that teenage readers would give a damning mark to, it was appealing solidly to that age group. However, and here was where the book really began to become a hit, it also was popular among older readers. 'People in their thirties, like me, have written me and told me that they can't stop reading it,' Meyer said. To an extent, this was surprising to her: 'I didn't realise the books would appeal to people so broadly.'

Lisa Hansen, a 36-year-old from Utah, is one such example of an older *Twilight* addict. 'I thought I was the only woman in the world who was my age and was just obsessed with books,' she told CNN. So she started a website called *Twilight Moms*, to which numerous *Twilight* fans 'of a certain age' flocked. 'The stigma of it being a teenager's book was the biggest issue,' Hansen said. 'Everyone felt the same way I did, like, "What's wrong with me? Why am I obsessing over this teenager thing?"'

Hansen was not alone. 'Many of us [fans] are happily married with kids, some as old as the male leads in *Twilight*. Some of them jokingly refer to themselves as "cougars" because of this, but it's used as a humorous way of saying we realize we are old enough to be [Edward actor] Robert Pattinson's mother [and] we still find him attractive,' said 49-year-old Patricia Kopicki.

However, some fans take the devotion to an even more explicit level. There is a *Twilight* blog in which older female fans discuss in vivid detail what they would like to do with the young male characters in Stephenie's books. 'We love to talk about how sexy Rob Pattinson is and what we would do if we got close,' said the blog's administrator. 'We feed off each other – we can be these racy, silly, just kind of goofy women about this. No one's being judged for being married and saying, "I'm 54 and I think this 23-year-old is absolutely delicious."'

All this bawdiness rather runs counter to the squeaky-clean approach Stephenie prefers to take to matters sexual in her novels. All the same, they have clearly struck a chord with their older female fanbase, for whom it has a special – and very welcome – appeal. 'It's a rekindling of old feelings, because when you're married and you've got kids and you're running around to the soccer and basketball and football games, [and you've got] work, bills . . . the relationship gets pushed off to the side,' explained Kopicki, who is a mother of two teenagers. 'Your husband may not look exactly like Edward, but just as men have their fantasies, women do too and they need to be able to express it,' she added. 'A book like *Twilight* has brought that out.'

For different age groups and genders, *Twilight* had pressed buttons. Quite a feat for Stephenie, a first-time author, to pull off. Although she sometimes protested that she found the mass appeal confusing, Stephenie eventually reasoned why this was happening. 'I think some of it's because Bella is an everyday girl. She's not a hero, and she doesn't even know the difference between Prada and whatever else is out there. She doesn't always have to be cool, or wear the coolest clothes ever. She's normal. And there aren't a lot of girls in literature that are normal. Another thing is that Bella's a good girl, which is just how I imagine teenagers, because that's how my teenage years were.'

Bella is the narrator of the story and – aside from one section of *Breaking Dawn* – the entire series. It was not a problem for Stephenie to do this. 'It was for me a very natural thing to write from a female perspective,' she insists. 'Because I wasn't thinking about what I was doing. I wasn't thinking, "Wow! I want to promote girl power." This was just for me. It was just a real natural thing and I'm glad that it's in the hands of a woman because I think you see things differently.

'I'm also glad that the male fanbase is building because we ladies grew up reading books through school that were written by men. We were assigned to read them, and you get the male perspective down pretty well. But boys don't always have to read books written by girls or see movies from that point of view, and I think it's just good for communication to have that interchange of ideas.'

Interesting, almost feminist speaking from Stephenie. Many *Twilight* fans and commentators have discussed with passion whether Bella can be considered a feminist hero. Proponents of this view point to her independent, steely nature and her love of books such as *Wuthering Heights*. She writes an essay in English class discussing whether or not Shakespeare is misogynistic. Others, though, counter that her unquestioning devotion to Edward – who does, let's remember, regularly crawl through the window into her bedroom at night as she sleeps – is far from a feminist example. 'I couldn't imagine anything about me that could be in any way interesting to him,' she says.

There are also moments that portray an old-fashioned view of the gender divide, such as when she comments that she would 'need to have Y chromosome' to understand the appeal of motorcycles. Nor does Bella have many relationships of any kind with people other than Edward – not the stuff of the inspirational modern woman.

However, writing on her website, Stephenie had dismissed the controversy. 'In my own opinion (key word), the foundation of feminism is this: being able to choose,' she writes. Seemingly in rejection of the motorcycle/Y chromosome accusation, she adds, 'The core of anti-feminism is, conversely, telling a woman she can't do something solely because she's a woman – taking any choice away from her specifically because of her gender.'

Warming to her theme, she continues, 'One of the weird things about modern feminism is that some feminists seem to be putting their own limits on women's choices. That feels backward to me. It's as if you can't choose a family on your own terms and still be considered a strong woman. How is that empowering? Are there rules about if, when, and how we love or marry and if, when, and how we have kids? Are there jobs we can and can't have in order to be a "real" feminist? To me, those limitations seem anti-feminist in basic principle.'

As Bidisha wrote in the *Independent* while assessing the entire four-book series, 'The problem – and there's no diplomatic way to say this – is that it's shockingly, tackily, sick-makingly sexist. Weak, inert, prone to falling over, crying and fainting, Bella Swan lives to serve men and suffer. When not cooking and cleaning for her father, she gapes with gratitude whenever

Edward saves her from harm and turns to querulous jelly when he's harsh – which is all the time. Edward stalks Bella for her own good, he says, prowling her house while she's asleep and making decisions for her. The series runs on Bella's thraldom to an undead jerk while the warmer character of Jacob Black, her werewolf best friend, lingers hopefully on the edges. It is depressing to read of a young woman who is treated like dirt for four books, yet faithfully worships Edward because of his hilariously clichéd "perfect face".'

Harsh words indeed, but they reflect the passion that Stephenie's work elicits from all parts of the spectrum. She takes all the criticism on the chin, realising that by putting out such powerfully popular stories she has to accept that people will have differing interpretations. As a passionate reader and opinionated woman herself, she cannot forbid others to have their own take on her body of work. She does, though, speak up for her hero Edward against those who have attacked or questioned him, arguing that he reflects noble human qualities that are not yet dead.

'The idea of a man being a gentleman has gone out of style,' she says. 'It's seen as old-world charm. People miss the fact that people are no longer considerate. Edward goes to great lengths so nothing bad happens to Bella, she is cared for so much. A lot of the book's appeal is the thought of being loved to that extent. There has been some antagonism from men about Edward. They are jealous because they don't want to try that hard.'

It is a vital point for her, not just about the story but about the real world. She adds, 'The media would like to tell us that boys can't help themselves, that there's an inbuilt sex drive so they can't hold themselves back, but there are so many great men out there, who make decisions based on moral standards. They do the right thing. Men like Edward do exist.' As for accusations that her stories are misogynistic, she says, 'I am not anti-female: I am anti-human.'

Normally a first-time author will have only modest promotional duties to fulfil for a novel. Nobody knows who the author is, so their presence at such events is not automatically required. With *Twilight* becoming a hit so quickly, Stephenie was thrown on to the promotional trail almost immediately. She was a first-time author facing the demands that only a far more experienced one would normally manage. She would learn on the hop the ways of press interviews, signing sessions, public readings and other launch events. One thing that struck her at some of these events was just how quickly she was picking up a dedicated fanbase. She would meet her most obsessive fans in person and hear over and over just how much they had enjoyed and connected with her story and characters. How moving it was to see first-hand their intense expressions and their declarations of devotion to Stephenie's characters! It was always the characters that meant most to her, too, so witnessing first-hand people's connections with them was warming vindication indeed. She found the attention and excitement overwhelming at times.

That said, the earliest events were sometimes attended by only modest numbers. For instance, in November 2005, she journeyed to Mequon in Wisconsin for an author appearance at the Harry W Schwartz bookshop on North Port Washington Road. Alongside her was the director of publicity for the book, Elizabeth Eulberg. Around a dozen people turned up, three of whom were the key *Twilight* demographic: teenage girls. Stephenie gave a speech to the audience, then opened up the discussion into a Q&A format. Finally, she signed copies of *Twilight* for those who attended. Some had brought extra copies to get signed. So far, it was a normal book-publicity session, plenty of which take place in bookshops across the world most nights of the year. However, after the event had ended and Stephenie had fulfilled all of her duties, she stayed back longer to talk to her fans. It was here that her common touch and humble nature shone through.

Stephenie stood for nearly an hour, talking to the fans who had stayed behind. She chatted to them, answered their questions and listened to their excited verdicts on and emotional connections with her works. Eulberg took some photographs of Stephenie with her fans and then she finally left, for the long drive home. However, Stephenie stayed in touch with the fans by email, even sending one of them the photograph that had been taken on the night. She communicated with them for months after the event, showing a willingness to speak to and engage with her fans that is rarely seen in authors. These fans, therefore, got to hear the latest news about Stephenie's career straight from the horse's mouth. 'Tomorrow I'm totally working on *New Moon*,' she wrote in one such message. 'So let it be written, so let it be done!'

Work was under way on the *Twilight* sequel, and Stephenie was not announcing it formally, but telling the fans about it – direct. She was becoming like the authorial equivalent of the British indie band Arctic Monkeys, who used the social networking website MySpace to promote themselves, largely cutting out the more traditional and formal methods, and the fans were responding.

Indeed, she was genuinely amazed by the lengths the fans would go to in order to meet her. 'One enthusiastic fan drove from Long Beach, California, to see me at a signing in Phoenix, Arizona, about a six-hour drive. Not only did she make the drive, she also brought me a giant Hello Kitty doll and, having read up on my obsessions on my website, a CD of my favourite band's B-side recordings. That CD is one of my most valued possessions.'

Her democratic, woman-of-the-people stance was admirable without a doubt. Many authors disappear into ivory towers and/or up their own behinds once fame comes their way. That Stephenie remained and remains as accessible as is possible and appropriate is to her credit. All the more so when you learn that she suffered major attacks of nerves before her public appearances in the early days. 'On that first tour, when I had to go to school events, I was throwing up before all of them. I was so scared – I was terrified of everything I had to do,' she remembered.

She also remained approachable online. When a fan wrote a 'fan fiction' piece from Edward Cullen's point of view and began to publish it online, she was shocked to receive some feedback from Stephenie herself. Included with the feedback was an offer from Stephenie to answer questions, if the fan had any. 'Well – DUH! Of course I had questions!' remembered the fan, who found that Stephenie replied generously. 'Basically from there on in, if I asked it, she answered it and then some. Oftentimes she would answer questions I hadn't even asked. It was as if she was begging to get this information out to her fans and at long last someone was willing to help.'

That correspondence in time led to the creation of the website *Twilight Lexicon*. This has become a formidable web presence, reflecting the awesome power and influence of Stephenie's writing ability.

The story was proving strangely, almost hypnotically, powerful – this despite the fact that it had been criticised in technical terms by many, including Stephenie herself.

So what was it about her vampire novel – inspired by a dream – that had struck such a chord with the reading public?

chapter four

the vampire effect

Deriving a novel from a dream is not an unheard-of experience for an author. It is believed that Mary Shelley's classic novel *Frankenstein, or the Modern Prometheus* was thus inspired. There are two such legends about the creation of that novel. According to the first, in 1815, Mary Shelley was in grief after her prematurely born baby had died before it was even a month old. Soon after her loss, she had a vivid dream that her baby came back to life. She recorded the dream in her diary on 19 March 1815, writing that 'it had only been cold and that we rubbed it before the fire and it lived'. From this dream, it is said, she first had the idea of a medical team creating a being and bringing it to life.

The other story goes that the following year, as she

holidayed in the Lake Geneva area, Shelley had a haunting 'waking dream' after Lord Byron had encouraged her to write a ghost story. She later revealed, 'I saw the pale student of unhallowed arts kneeling beside the thing he had put together. I saw the hideous phantasm of a man stretched out, and then, on the working of some powerful engine, show signs of life, and stir with an uneasy, half-vital motion. Frightful must it be; for supremely frightful would be the effect of any human endeavour to mock the stupendous Creator of the world.'

Stephenie would be just as affected by what she saw in her sleep two centuries later.

Meanwhile, later in the 19th century, another novel that was destined for classic status came into being as a result of an author's dream. Scottish writer Robert Louis Stevenson was asleep one evening in the autumn of 1885 when a couple of scenes came into his imagination. He might have dreamed more scenes had his wife not interrupted his sleep.

'In the small hours of one morning,' said Mrs Stevenson, 'I was awakened by cries of horror from Louis. Thinking he had a nightmare, I woke him. He said angrily, "Why did you wake me? I was dreaming a fine bogey tale." I had awakened him at the first transformation scene . . .'

Nonetheless, he had dreamed enough to inspire him to start writing a new story on a theme that had fascinated him for some time. 'I had long been trying to write a story on that strong sense of man's double being,' he said. 'For two days I went about racking my brains for a plot of any sort; and on the second night I dreamed the scene at the window, and a scene afterwards split in two, in which Hyde, pursued for some crime, took the powder and underwent the change in the presence of his pursuers.'

The result was *The Strange Case of Dr Jekyll and Mr Hyde*, an enormously successful and influential novella that continues to be a popular tale to this very day.

Many other authors say they are frequently inspired by dreams, including horror novelist (and critic of Stephenie) Stephen King. Jacquelyn Mitchard, author of *The Deep End of the Ocean* – a novel about a mother whose three-year-old child is kidnapped – was also thus struck. 'I dreamed the story about three years ago. For a year after that I didn't do anything with it beyond the notes I made about the dream. I'd never written a novel before, but the dream was clear and astonishing. And I'm not much of a dreamer in the ordinary sense.'

Samuel Coleridge composed his poem 'Kubla Khan' while in an opium-fuelled dream state. Supremely influential, though, was the effect of Shelley's endeavour to turn her dream (or the previous dream, or a combination of the two) into a fictional story. Not unlike Stephenie, Shelley began writing the resulting story tentatively. She thought it might be at most a short story. However, it turned into a novel, which then grabbed the public imagination at a time that scientists were discussing the possibility of bringing corpses back to life using electricity. In the 1820s, the story was adapted for stage. It has since been featured in cartoon, cinematic and theatrical form and continues to be so to this day. True, it has at times been misunderstood and many believe that the monster – rather than its creator – is the Frankenstein of the story. Also, the image some have of the monster as inherently evil is incorrect. Nonetheless, its influence cannot be doubted.

Nor can the influence and presence of Stephenie's chosen character – the vampire – on prevailing culture. For centuries, the vampire has been an immensely popular figure, spreading its influence from poetry to novels, to film, television and comic strips. It has also been a favourite in art, theatre and music. With Stephenie giving the vampire a renaissance on both the printed page and the big screen, the public show absolutely no sign of tiring of the genre just yet.

But what is behind our fascination with vampires? Where did it come from, and what does it say about us? Stephenie herself is, strangely, not claiming to have an expert answer herself. 'I have never gotten it – why are people obsessed with vampires, you know?' she said. 'And I know a lot of people who are. I'm actually surprised now I know how many more people are, and so the fact I would write about them is wildly out of character for me and bizarre, and nobody who knows me believed it for a really long time.'

As we shall see, she is not without her own theory, but first let's trace the history of the public's fascination with vampires and chew over some of the main theories for their popularity.

The first vampire character to grab the public by the scruff of the neck, and the most infamous one to this day is Dracula, who is the titular hero of a novel written by Bram Stoker in 1897. The book is composed of a series of letter and diary entries, together with occasional fictional newspaper cuttings. The protagonist of the story is Count Dracula, a vampire who inhabits a sorry castle in the now legendary Transylvania. With an aristocratic air about him, he easily deceives people and becomes perhaps the greatest predator in literary history.

As the story develops, he traps a British lawyer in his castle and then torments the people of Britain. An unattended ship is destroyed, bite marks appear on a woman's neck and plenty more until a team is formed to try to counter his menace, setting up a fabulous conclusion. He is tracked back to his castle and set upon by the team, who attack him with knives, leaving him crumbling to dust, providing a dramatic conclusion to a gripping story.

Many of the readers of Victorian England highly enjoyed the novel when it came out, and it received favourable reviews from the critics too. The *Daily Mail* wrote, 'In seeking a parallel to this weird, powerful, and horrorful story our mind reverts to such tales as *The Mysteries of Udolpho*, *Frankenstein*, *The Fall of the House of Usher* . . . but *Dracula* is even more appalling in its gloomy fascination than any one of these.'

It was also well received in America, where it was published two years later to widespread admiration. However, it was not until the following century that the vampire character of Dracula truly sank its fangs into the public cultural consciousness when the story was taken to a new medium. In 1924, Hamilton Deane was given permission by Stoker's wife to adapt the novel for the stage. Then, three years later, that version was revised by John L Balderston. It toured the UK and eventually stayed in London for a prolonged run. It was then taken to America, where it played on New York's legendary Broadway to terrified yet delighted packed houses. Bela Lugosi famously played the title role. The production won numerous awards, but its greatest legacy was felt in the world of cinema.

It was in 1931 that the film version of the Dracula story hit the big screens. In a film directed by Tod Browning, Lugosi was chosen for the title role once more, but not before the filmmakers had searched hard for someone else to take the part. While it was being made, a Spanish version was being shot, each scene being filmed twice with each cast and language alternating. Interestingly, the scene in the story when Dracula attacks a man was cut for fears that it implied a gay subtext to the character. 'Dracula is only to attack women,' read a memo handed to the director by the movie house. The sexual undercurrents of the story were, reportedly, mirrored in real life. Bram Stoker is thought by some to have suffered from syphilis. This is not mentioned here flippantly: as we shall see, some commentators have speculated that that fact was important in the creation of the character.

It premiered on 21 February 1931 at the Roxy Theater in New York City. Lugosi was fantastic in the role, with a fine way of delivering lines slowly and a face so pale that it added to the sense that this was a real manifestation of a living-dead vampire. 'I – never – drink – wine,' he said chillingly. Indeed, so scared did audiences become that, within a few years of the film's release, some of the more frightening scenes were cut and the film would be followed by a brief message to reassure cinemagoers, as had been added to the end of the *Frankenstein* movie previously. The toning down of the film did nothing to stop its popularity and, in the wake of the film's first showing, the press reported that audience members had fainted in shock at the chilling tale. People flocked to the cinema to watch the film, which prompted the dawn of the horror genre in the movie industry. And it all started with Stoker's novel, although, to be strictly accurate, that had not been the first instance of vampirism in literature by any means.

Interestingly, during the aforementioned trip to Lake Geneva made in 1816 by Mary Shelley, which prompted her to write *Frankenstein*, two more works were inspired among those who were holidaying with her. John William Polidori wrote a short story called *The Vampyre*, which is widely credited with having kicked off the vampire genre in literature. Popular-culture academic Sir Christopher Frayling has described the tale as 'the first story successfully to fuse the disparate elements of vampirism into a coherent literary genre'. That said, there had been a poem published as early as 1773 that touched on vampirism.

Polidori's story follows a young Englishman who becomes entangled in the life of a shadowy character called Lord Ruthven, who turns out to be a vampire. The story concludes with Ruthven marrying and then killing the sister of the young Englishman. This is the first significant recorded appearance of a vampire in a fictional book, and its influence was quickly and keenly felt in the literary world. The Ruthven character is thought to have been modelled on Lord Byron, who was also present during the Lake Geneva trip and who wrote his own horror story in the wake of the trip. The story, later published under the title *Fragment of a Novel*, was never completed by Byron, but it is widely believed that he intended to introduce vampire characters and themes to the story before his own death robbed him of the chance to complete the work.

The fascination was to continue, nonetheless. In the middle of the 19th century, more vampire works appeared on the bookshelves. James Malcolm Rymer

Stephenie Meyer signs copies of *Twilight*, the first book in her best-selling series.

Above: Stephenie with Catherine Hardwicke, the director of the *Twilight* movie, sign posters for fans at Comic-Con 2008.

Below: The cast of *Twilight* join with Stephenie and Catherine for the perfect Comic-Con photo-op.

Above: Stephenie hosted the *Breaking Dawn* Concert Series for the launch of the fourth and final book in *The Twilight Saga*.

Below: On stage with Justin Furstenfeld, of the band Blue October, whose lyrics and music helped to inspire Stephenie's writing.

Stephenie and her husband
Christiaan, nicknamed 'Pancho', at
the premiere of *Twilight*.

Above: Bombarded by fans at the *Twilight* premiere.

Below: Posing with Edi Gathegi and Peter Facinelli (Laurent and Carlisle in *Twilight*).

Stephenie's beloved characters come to life on screen.

Above: Kristen Stewart and Robert Pattinson as the perfect Bella Swan and Edward Cullen.

Below: Taylor Lautner worked hard to realise Stephenie's vision for Jacob Black.

Above: Signing for fans at *The Twilight Saga: New Moon* premiere.

Below left: Stephenie Meyer looking glamorous with red lips and a stunning embellished fishtail dress.

Below right: Dakota Fanning (who plays Jane of the Volturi) and Kristen Stewart (Bella) also adorned the red carpet.

Stephenie beaming at the premiere of
The Twilight Saga: New Moon. The future looks
bright for the world's most beloved author.

had written a series of horror story in the form of 'penny dreadfuls'. These were pamphlets that published, at the price of one penny a time, a series of lurid, horror stories. They were primarily aimed at teenage readers. Rymer's stories were then collated into one single publication called *Varney The Vampire or The Feast of Blood*. The titular character, Varney, set the blueprint for the vampire's representation in novels. He had fangs and would bite his victims on the neck, and had hypnotic, supernatural powers. Varney would also come through a window to confront a female victim, a modified version of which occurs throughout the *Twilight* series, when Edward regularly visits Bella by coming through the window of her bedroom at night. Varney was also perhaps the first 'reluctant' vampire character. His influence was immense, even being noticed in the Marvel Comics series, the creators of which named their first ever vampire character 'Varnae' after Rymer's character.

In 1872, the first erotically based vampire novel was released. Irish writer John Sheridan Le Fanu wrote *Carmilla*, the tale of a young woman who garners the attention of a female vampire. This was not the sort of story that would hold much appeal for Stephenie. The titular heroine of the story could pass through walls and slept in a coffin. The lesbian nature of the story was not explicit, but was clear to most savvy readers.

Some of the story is thought to have been based on an 18th-century essay written by Antoine Augustin

Calmet, a monk who wrote about the possibility that vampires really existed. In turn, *Carmilla*'s influence was seen keenly in the novel *Dracula*, which, as we have seen, quickly became the definitive work on the vampire. So successful and authoritative was the book that it drew something of a line in the development of the genre. Few authors even tried to bring anything new to the party for some time after *Dracula*, and for a while the vampire looked set to die out in the literary world. It was not until deep into the 20th century that new ideas began to be injected into vampire fiction. A second golden age of the literary bloodsucker was about to sink its fangs into the public consciousness.

The signpost novel in this new era of the vampire as a science-fiction concern came in 1954 with *I Am Legend* by American writer Richard Matheson. The story is best known by modern readers for the cinematic adaptation (one of many) starring Will Smith. It started life as a novel, though, in which a post-apocalyptic world has been almost destroyed by a disease that includes vampire elements. The idea of vampires being the result of a scientific occurrence was still a new one at this stage and Matheson's story was key in kicking off what is now a familiar trend.

Then came *Doctors Wear Scarlet* in 1960, in which vampirism is based not in Transylvania but Greece. In the 1970s, Stephen King joined the vampire trend when he published *Salem's Lot*. In his story vampires take over a town in Maine and cause havoc. It had been influenced by the landmark vampire that is Dracula.

'One night over supper I wondered aloud what would happen if Dracula came back in the 20th century, to America,' remembered King. He later added, 'I began to turn the idea over in my mind, and it began to coalesce into a possible novel. I thought it would make a good one, if I could create a fictional town with enough prosaic reality about it to offset the comic-book menace of a bunch of vampires.'

King's influence can be seen in the work of George R R Martin, who wrote *Fevre Dream*, which is about seagoing vampirism. Then, in 1976, Anne Rice began to publish a series of books known as *The Vampire Chronicles*, which echoed some of the erotic themes we had seen in *Carmilla*. These have become extremely popular and influential works: an original copy of one of Rice's novels recently sold for £750 online. (It should be noted, though, that this figure is dwarfed by the money that changes hands for original copies of *Dracula*. Stoker's novel commands sums comfortably into five figures for original editions.) As we shall see, the Rice series' most keenly felt influence was seen on the big screen two decades later.

Sherrilyn Kenyon is a more recent author to rule the roost. Her *Dark-Hunter* vampire series of works has become enormously popular. They feature immortal warriors who battle on behalf of a Greek goddess to fight against sinister enemies, primarily vampires. She has developed a keen international following and her fanbase is committed to say the least. Fan conventions for Kenyon's works are huge and paved the way for the sort of hysterical fandom that we have seen erupt around Stephenie Meyer in more recent times.

Soon after Kenyon had begun to see her work take off, more romantic vampire works started to hit the bestseller lists. Christine Feehan tackled vampires via the romantic route in her 'dark series' of novels, which kicked off with *Dark Prince* in 1999. *Anita Blake: Vampire Hunter* by Laurell K Hamilton also concerned vampire characters, and used a similar angle. Here, the vampire story was being brought to an increasingly female audience, as it was by *The Moth Diaries*, published by Rachel Klein.

However, things would swing dramatically more in that direction when Stephenie put pen to paper the following century. Politics has often been injected into the blood-life of the vampire story. *Fangland* is a post-9/11 take on the *Dracula* theme and *Suckers* by Anne Billson – complete with a vivid menstruation scene – was praised as a satire on the perceived greed of the 1980s yuppie era.

Since the 1930s, the Dracula character has become an iconic one in popular culture and has blazed the cinematic trail that the big-screen adaptations of Stephenie's books now dominate. More than 200 films have been made that feature Count Dracula as a character and hundreds more make a reference to him.

Meanwhile, thousands of other cultural works have been made with a Dracula theme including novels, cartoons, ballet, television shows and songs. Computer games, too, have often included him as a participant.

There are even Dracula-themed holidays, in places such as Ireland, Britain and Romania. As a result of this trend, Dracula has become as familiar a cultural character as the great detective Sherlock Holmes. He is the character who put the vampire not merely *on* the cultural map but right in the centre of it. He had not, though, been the subject of the first ever vampire film. As early as 1909, a silent movie called *Vampire of the Coast* was released and, in 1922, *Nosferatu* came out. This was a thinly veiled and unauthorised adaptation of Stoker's novel. But it was only with the dawn of the official *Dracula* movie that the character – and with it the vampire – truly entered the public psyche. Without him, Stephenie would not have dreamed of the meadow scene, there would have been no Edward Cullen and there would have been no *Twilight* series. However, there would be a lot of other developments in the vampire story before Edward Cullen joined Count Dracula on the cultural map.

Following a pair of sequels to Count Dracula's story (*Dracula's Daughter* in 1936 and *Son of Dracula* in 1943), the character then began to appear in films made by the Hammer Horror house. The first was released in 1958, starring Christopher Lee as the vampiric protagonist. He also took the lead in five of the seven subsequent sequels. The 1960s saw the genre broaden out with the first lesbian vampire film (*Blood and Rose*, 1960) and a glut of vampire comedies including *The Fearless Vampire Killers* (1967). A more recent instance of this vampire-parody genre is 1995's *Dracula: Dead and Loving It*, which was directed by Mel Brooks and stars Leslie Nielsen. Sandwiched between these were numerous vampire films that include David Cronenberg's *Rabid*. Released in 1977, it portrayed vampirism not as a supernatural occurrence but rather a virus.

In 1987, a more youth-orientated vampire film was released. *The Lost Boys* came with the zesty strapline, 'Sleep all day. Party all night. Never grow old. Never die. It's fun to be a vampire.' It focuses on two teenage brothers who, when the family move to a new coastal town in California, become convinced that the area is populated by vampires. One brother begins to show the signs of vampirism and the younger brother consequently teams up with two vampire hunters to try to save his elder sibling. It coined a new phrase in popular culture: 'vamp out'.

The most influential vampire films of the latter 20th century were released in the 1990s. If the 1930s was the first explosion of the vampire in cinema, then the 1990s saw the aftershock. Towards the end of the first decade of the 21st century, a third golden era of vampire movies occurred. Many of those who watched it were still in nappies during the 1990s vampire-fest.

As for Stephenie, she moved from her teens into her twenties during that decade. Although she says she never saw any vampire films because she was too scared to, she would have been aware of their prominence in the world of cinema, and in that sense they were having an influence on her. John Landis directed *Innocent Blood*, which hit the big screen in 1992. With this film the genre was tied to the gangster theme. Featuring actors who would later find television mobster superstardom in *The Sopranos*, it focused on a female vampire (played by Anne Parillaud) who is tormented by bloodsucking gangsters.

It had a darkly comedic element to it, as did *Vampire in Brooklyn*, which was released in 1995. It starred Eddie Murphy and Angela Bassett, and was directed by Wes Craven. Murphy's character is the last in a line of vampires, and stalks Brooklyn looking for a mate to continue the line with. There was a tension behind the scenes because Craven and Murphy had differing visions of how the final product would look. The previous year had seen the release of the big-screen adaptation of the aforementioned Anne Rice's 1976 novel *Interview with the Vampire*. As one of *The Vampire Chronicles*, it starred Brad Pitt and Tom Cruise. Although controversy surrounded the casting of Cruise – not least from Rice, who objected publicly, saying the actor was 'no more my Vampire Lestat than Edward G Robinson is Rhett Butler' – he played the part of the brooding vampire very well in the eyes of many, including Rice, who retracted her protests. A similar reaction would be made by Stephenie to one of the key casting points in the adaptations of her own vampire novels.

Next came the *Buffy the Vampire Slayer* television series. Following the 1992 movie of the same name, *Buffy the Vampire Slayer* aired first on America's WB network. It followed the fortunes of Buffy (played by Sarah Michelle Gellar), who is a member of the Slayer line of females who fight vampires, demons and other creatures. She had a gang of loyal friends known as the 'Scooby Gang'.

Buffy the Vampire Slayer became a hugely significant and influential cultural moment. With a huge fanbase, it became a regular subject in academic popular-culture studies. Among its fans was Stephenie's sister Emily. Coinciding, as the series did, with the mainstream explosion of the Internet, it picked up a huge cult online following and many fans made their own unofficial 'fan film' versions of the story. It has been referenced in numerous other cultural outlets, including sketch shows on both sides of the Atlantic and in television comedies, including *Friends*, *Will and Grace* and the smash-hit cartoon series *The Simpsons*. Even video games have paid homage to the *Buffy* franchise, including references in *Grand Theft Auto IV* and *The Burning Crusade*. If any vampire-related character (prior to the emergence of Edward Cullen) threatened to knock Dracula off his bloodsucking perch, that that was Buffy.

The series even spawned its own lexicon, which was absorbed and adopted by its legion of fans. If something was 'carbon-dated', it meant it was very out of date and a 'cuddle monkey' was a male lover. It has also influenced subsequent stories in *Doctor Who* and its spin-off series *Torchwood*. Again, it seems highly likely that Stephenie was aware of the show and – given its relative lack of frightening scenes – may have watched an episode or two. However, as it included some sexual content (some of it deemed worthy of censorship by the BBC during its transmission of the sixth series), it would not have been a show she would have made much noise about watching among her Mormon pals.

Since she published the *Twilight* series and then saw them secure cinematic deals, the world has gone vampire mad again, just as it did in the 1990s. *Thirst* hit the big screens in the autumn of 2009. Made by South Korean 'master of macabre' Park Chan-Wook, it is a dark, violent and sexual tale of vampires who make anything that happens in the *Twilight* series seem positively twee in comparison. For instance, one character while playing his flute begins to vomit blood, which goes into the instrument and spurts out of the tone holes.

The same year saw *Cirque du Freak: The Vampire's Assistant*, which follows a teenage boy who meets a man who, it soon transpires, is a vampire. The boy then joins the circus and becomes a vampire himself.

Similarly to *Twilight*, it is based on a series of novels and has a strong teen appeal. It hit the big screens in the UK just weeks before the *New Moon* film came to town. The vampires in *Cirque du Freak* are not evil creatures but essentially harmless. The star of the film, Josh Hutcherson, is convinced that *Cirque*'s vampires have the edge on those of *Twilight*. 'We're a whole different thing,' he boasted. 'We'll kill *Twilight*. We'll eat those guys alive. We're a lot cooler than them!' (He was, though, balanced enough to admit that Robert Pattinson of the *Twilight* films outsexed the *Cirque* cast.)

So what is behind our enduring love of the vampire, be it on the big screen, the printed page or a combination of the two? Theories have been discussed for some time, and a few key ones have gathered weight. Some commentators says that vampires are linked to times of financial woe. They point out that *Dracula* emerged in celluloid form in the 1930s, a time of financial depression. (*Twilight* series character Rosalie's human life also took place during the era.) Then, with Stephenie's *Twilight* series prompting a second wave of vampire popularity in the first decade of the 21st century, some made a connection between this trend and the dark cloud of financial depression that hung over the world. Could this be a coincidence? asked proponents of this theory. In short, the answer was yes, it could be. While this theory is not without some evidence, it falls far short of being a definitive answer to the popularity of the genre that has also thrived at times of comparative financial confidence. Other political interpretations of the vampire have centred on Dracula's being a representation of the Ancien Régime in 14th-century France. As we shall see, Stephenie largely steers clear of politics, though there were political themes in a short story she wrote in 2007.

Then there is the theory that it all comes down to one thing – sex. Indeed, the 1990s' wave of vampire films, it is argued, was mainly Hollywood's way of dealing with the AIDS issue. Blood being drawn, infections being passed round, it seemed that the obsession with vampires in the first full decade of the AIDS phenomenon was no coincidence. Some people believe that the 1995 film *The Addiction*, directed by Abel Ferrara, was set in New York and referenced AIDS and drug use. Syringes were brandished as weapons and the dark metropolitan imagery was certainly connecting of AIDS and vampirism. However, other critics say that the film had little to do with bloodshed and vampirism, or AIDS, and is more a warning about the immediate perils of drug addiction.

Still, the movie-business wisdom remains that couples like watching scary films together, because, it is argued, those moments of terror are effective aphrodisiacs. Stephenie's restrained, abstinence-ruled stories rather contradict this view, though some say that it is precisely the resultant sexual tension that confirms it.

Her own theory is rather more simple – some people enjoy being terrified. 'This is my theory, having talked to a lot of people about why do you like vampires so much?' says the author with little interest in vampires as a reader but an enormous one as a writer. 'Besides myself, it seems like everybody really loves to be scared in a controlled environment. Horror movies do really well, you know? It's a big industry. People read a lot of scary books. So I'm missing that gene, but clearly we like to be scared and they look at the monsters we can scare ourselves with and most of them are disgusting and, you know, gruesome, and they're covered in nasty things. And we don't want anything from them. We just want to get away from them. They're just there to scare us.

'And then we've got vampires who are often beautiful and eternally youthful and rich and cultured and they live in castles. There are so many things that are ideals in our culture that we want that they have, so there's this double-edged sword – they're going to kill us and they're terrifying and yet maybe I even want to be one. I don't want to be a vampire. A lot of other people do and I think it's that dual nature we have – you know, terrifying/intriguing.'

Even though in her leisure time she is not turned on by the vampire thing, Stephenie really knows her stuff about the cultural history of these beings – and where her own characters fit into the tradition. 'Well, in general, because I know there's a lot of varying legends, you know, and there's the ones that turn into bats and mist and there's the ones that are more concrete,' she says. 'In general, my vampires don't have fangs and they don't need them. You know, strong as they are, it's kind of unnecessary. They're fairly indestructible. Wooden stakes and garlic are not going to get you anywhere. They don't sleep at all, they're never unconscious, they have no periods of unconsciousness. And the sunlight doesn't harm them, it just shows them for what they are because they sparkle in the sun.'

So these were Stephenie's vampires, created from a dream she had one night. They differed from many of their bloodsucking antecedents, but the public were loving them. She was ready to give us more of what we wanted with a spectacular return to the bookshelves with another vampire novel, the second in the *Twilight* trilogy.

Having written the 'hundred-page epilogues' to *Twilight* in the wake of completing that story, Stephenie Meyer began to fashion the plot into a whole new novel – *New Moon*. After the speedy and relatively painless process of writing *Twilight*, it seems that the follow-up came with rather more strain for Stephenie. She has even compared it to the process of childbirth. 'It's equal in pain, and can drag on and on,' she said. During the writing process she found herself working on two separate manuscripts at one point, which made for complications. 'I've been making editorial changes in both places,' she said. 'I'm going to have to print both out so I can lay the pages side by side to find the differences and choose the ones I like best.'

Just as with *Twilight*, she found music very important to the writing process. For this book she became increasingly fond of and inspired by the music of the Los Angeles band Marjorie Fair. 'For *New Moon* they were absolutely essential,' enthused Stephenie. 'They can put you into a suicidal state faster than anything I know. It's just this heartbreaking music where the pain is done so beautifully. It really got me in the zone for writing about a person who is horribly depressed and yet not at all showing it. She's not wearing black and refusing to come out of her room and yelling at the people she loves. She is completely containing it inside herself. Their songs really made it beautiful for me.'

Happily, amid the pain and strain, some passages of *New Moon* were joyfully easy to create for Stephenie. 'The scene in Volterra [in Italy], that scene came very, very freely to me, and that's some of my favourite writing in that scene; it came like a movie to me and I just wrote it down as that scene. I like that a lot.'

However, the ending of the story was nearly very different from the one greedily devoured by her fans – and a lot more tame. For the fact that this ending was never published, Stephenie can thank her ever-interested mother.

'There was a different ending *to New Moon*,' the author recalls. 'It was a much quieter book. I was telling my mom about it . . . and my mom's like, "Y'know, Stephenie, maybe a little more action at the end would be a good idea . . ." And she was right, as usual . . . I introduced the Volturi [an ancient vampire family] a little bit earlier in the series than I was planning . . . It's kind of like my favourite part now.'

Mother knows best, Stephenie!

The public were to enjoy the book a lot when it appeared on their shelves. After the apple of *Twilight*, the cover concept this time was a ruffled tulip, with one petal falling from the flower. It made for a striking and beautiful image, but the significance of it is lost on Stephenie.

'The apple cover [for *Twilight*] had a lot of meaning for me, and I was an active part of the covering process,' she wrote on her personal website. 'However, that experience is more the exception than the rule in the publishing world. Something to keep in mind if you intend to embark on a career as a writer: lots of things you might expect to be under your control are not. Covers, for example. Those are mostly up to the publisher and the marketing and sales departments. So I don't know what the tulip means – I didn't have anything to do with this one.'

Instead, she had suggested that the cover concept should include a clock image, to tie in – one assumes – with the clock tower in the centre of Volterra.

However, it was the tulip image that they went for. As for the title *New Moon*, this had nothing to do with any werewolf theme. 'The term "new moon" refers to the phase of the moon opposite a full moon,' explains Stephenie. 'It is when the sun is on the opposite side of the moon from us and thus the bright side of the moon is not visible from earth. This is the darkest kind of night. *New Moon* is the darkest period of Bella's life.'

The book hit the shelves on 6 September 2006. A hundred thousand copies were initially printed (up from the 75,000 copies that formed the initial print run for *Twilight*, reflecting the growth in popularity and confidence). With the book published, it was time for the reviewers to deliver their verdicts. This was an intriguing time for Stephenie. The first book had been such an unexpected smash hit that some reviewers were rather caught on the hop by it. Given that the book-review world is ruled by political considerations as much as by the actual content of the works being reviewed, this could lead to one of two trends in the reception for *New Moon*. It could lead to reviewers showering the book with praise, all the better to 'get in with' the *Twilight* bandwagon. Or it could lead to reviewers giving it an especially rough ride, as part of a 'great backlash' against a franchise that they might cynically feel was getting too big for its boots. All Stephenie could hope was that they were fair with her book, which had been at times a tricky project to complete. It is not just that a good review can help a book commercially, though that is obviously a concern for all involved in the book. It is also that authors such as Stephenie are often on tenterhooks waiting to see what people will make of their work, which has been a labour of some love for them.

As is often the case with novels from big-name American authors, one of the earliest verdicts came from *Kirkus Reviews*. This is an influential publication that reviews books prior to their release and is therefore seen as landmark in its verdicts. The review was upbeat and admiring. The article said, 'Psychic miscommunications and angst-ridden dramatic gestures lead to an exciting page-turner of a conclusion drenched in the best of Gothic romantic excess. Despite Bella's flat and obsessive personality, this tale of tortured demon lovers entices.'

Kirkus can set the tone for a book's reception, so a thumbs-up from it was important. Ahead of the main wave of reviews came another from a book-trade journal, as *Publishers' Weekly* emerged from the critical traps. This magazine, which had so praised *Twilight*, took a more negative and cautionary tone. 'Fans of Meyer's debut novel, *Twilight*, may be disappointed in this second book in a planned trilogy . . . Long stretches in the book may make readers feel as if they're treading water.'

With the trade press giving the book a mixed reception, Stephenie had one soaringly positive verdict and one decidedly negative one as she awaited the main round of receptions from the big American newspapers. The giant *USA Today* regretted the lack of vampires in the sequel, but still found much to praise in *New Moon*. 'Meyer's narrative is heavier on teen drama than supernatural activity, yet perhaps that's what has made her tales such must-haves for young readers,' wrote Whitney Matheson. '*New Moon* piles on the suspense and romance, but if it's blood-sucking one craves, you won't find it here.'

The *New York Times* enjoyed her trick of representing Bella's despair after the disappearance of Edward. 'Meyer perfectly conveys [Bella's] depression with a series of pages that are blank except for the names of passing months – October, November, December,' it beamed. 'Fans will be almost as impatient for Edward's return, but tough and resourceful Bella is the star of this book.'

Booklist was measured in its praise. 'The writing is a bit melodramatic,' judged Cindy Dobrez. 'But readers won't care. Bella's dismay at being ordinary (after all, she's only human) will strike a chord even among girls who have no desire to be immortal, and like the vampires who watch Bella bleed with "fevered eyes", teens will relish this new adventure and hunger for more.'

Proof for Stephenie that you just can't please 'em all came with the write-up of *New Moon* published by the *San Jose Mercury News*. The newspaper accused her of 'clumsy writing' and said that she 'practically hits readers over the head with her aggravating comparisons of the two main characters to Romeo and Juliet!' It took an opposite stance to the *New York Times* on the way Stephenie represented Bella's despair as it continued, 'What's even more irritating is Bella's drawn-out, melodramatic zombie state during Edward's absence.' However the review concluded positively, saying, '*New Moon* is a quintessential teen book. Its themes and situations are timeless, only with an intriguingly dark twist.'

As Stephenie would increasingly discover, her books rarely form any sort of critical consensus. This is surely a good thing that reflects well on her work, however irritating or hurtful the negative comments might be to her.

As with *Twilight*, the American publication *School Library Journal* had its say on this YA (young-adult) novel. A positive say it was, too: 'Fans of *Twilight* won't be disappointed, and those new to the series can pick it up here and go back later to find out more about Edward's evil co-vampires.'

The Oregon newspaper *Eugene Weekly* memorably headed its review 'Bloody Glorious', and described the book as 'über-romantic, torridly overwritten yet highly compelling to older teens'.

The *Chicago Tribune* had university professor Mary Harris Russell run her eyes over the book. The specialist's verdict was that it was 'full of the same wit and pacing' as *Twilight*, adding that 'the action moves fast in this combination of genre plotting and witty fun'.

On and on the verdicts came, showing in their sheer number how important a figure Stephenie was becoming. *VOYA* (Voice of Youth Advocates, a magazine devoted to young adults) said of *New Moon*, 'Vampire aficionados will voraciously consume this mighty tome in one sitting, then flip back and read it once more. It maintains a brisk pace and near-genius balancing of breathtaking romance and action.'

Another magazine's review concluded that the sequel was: 'Less streamlined than *Twilight* yet just as exciting, [it] will more than feed the bloodthirsty hankerings of fans of the first volume and leave them breathless for a third.'

Before that third edition arrived, though, Stephenie would deliver a short story about demons. Amid her soaring popularity and critical esteem, she had often been accused of being unable to pull off brevity in her writing. Squeezed into the shortest prose fiction form, how would she fare? And what mischief would her demons get up to?

chapter five

prom nights and bright lights

In April 2007, Stephenie Meyer's second short story was published, following her short-form debut *Hero At The Grocery Store*, which was quietly published the previous year in a Mormon magazine called *Ensign*. *Prom Nights from Hell* was a collection of five short stories written by well-known authors. Joining Stephenie in the team were Meg Cabot, author of *How To Be Popular* and *The Princess Diaries*, Kim Harrison (*Once Dead, Twice Shy*); Michele Jaffe (*The Stargazer*) and Lauren Myracle (*Love Yah Bunches*). Each wrote a short story around the theme of a prom night that went wrong in a paranormal way. It was published by HarperCollins. As the accompanying publicity put it, 'Wardrobe malfunctions and two left feet don't hold a candle to discovering your date is the Grim Reaper – and he isn't here to tell you how hot you look. From angels fighting demons to a creepy take on getting what you wish for, these five stories will entertain better than any DJ in a bad tux. No corsage or limo rental necessary. Just good, scary fun.'

It was also good charitable fun. A portion of the proceeds for each copy of the book sold went to the First Book nonprofit organisation. First Book is a cause close to Stephenie's heart, and it works to give children from poor families the chance to own and read their own first book. She is, as we shall see throughout her story, a very generous woman. For instance, it is rumoured that she gives away a portion of her income to her local LDS church. The figure is believed to be 10 per cent of her earnings each year.

Stephenie's story in the collection was called 'Hell on Earth' and it closed the book – in some style, too. For the reader accustomed to Stephenie's novels, the pace of her short story is surprising – it leaves one feeling almost dizzy. With the pace sped up, she also loses some of her inhibitions about sexual passion. On only the second page, she describes a snogging couple by saying one had 'lost something she needed deep inside Heath's mouth'. Vivid stuff, and a turn of phrase one would not expect in a *Twilight* book.

The story covers some demons who are secretly wreaking havoc at a school prom on a humid night in Miami, Florida. One of them spreads chaos among the students as she walks. As she passes them they lose a contact lens, or break a high heel or have an unexpectedly early period – 'little disasters spinning small circles of misery'. Her imagery is vivid: one character notices a boy's 'coffee eyes swimming with tears'. Later she writes, 'Like a rubber band that had been stretched too far, the atmosphere . . . now snapped back with a vengeance.' One character realises that he has a gun on him, 'like he'd just woken from a dream', she writes with the soporific theme emerging again.

In this story Stephenie takes a more political turn than had been seen from her work before or since. One of the demons tells the other that their mission to spread evil was one it was 'obvious we're winning'. But even with all the war and destruction in the world, counters the other, there are always good things too. For every successful mugging there is another where a hero intervenes. 'We're losing ground,' complains the demon.

In truth, this is not heavily political or at all partisan stuff, but it does mark the most overtly social commentary that Stephenie has made to date. Her prom story – and therefore the book itself – ends up with a positive outlook. When one demon 'celebrates' that misery is everywhere, the sibling demon counters, 'Happiness is too, sis. It's all over the place.' There is also humour. In commenting on the hot, sticky night, a demon says, 'Miami was no hell but it was comfortable at least.'

A woman who openly admits that she finds brevity

difficult, Stephenie will have been nervous of how the story would be received. This was the first non-*Twilight* work of hers to be widely reviewed and at the time only the fourth piece of work she had published, following *Twilight* and *New Moon*. Thankfully for her, the reception for the *Prom Nights From Hell* book and her contribution to it were largely positive. 'Far from gauzy clichés, the prom nights depicted in this anthology are surreal and often populated with monsters and zombies,' wrote Gillian Enberg in *Booklist*. 'The tone in each story wavers between glib camp and chilling terror, just like a teen horror movie. Like many anthologies, this one is uneven, but there is plenty to amuse older horror fans, particularly those with a cynical view of prom night.'

Stephenie must have a highly cynical view of prom night, judging by the disastrous hurtful behaviour that is rampant in her story. Whether there's a demon being exorcised in her writing of the story, only she and her prom date KJ could say. They were certainly all smiles in the photograph taken before they left for the prom. One wonders what happened once they got there.

The verdicts were plentiful for the book, given Stephenie's involvement in it. Other reviewers have praised the collection. 'Sure to have appeal for older teens, this book will undoubtedly make the circuit of fans of demons, ghosts, vampires, and gothic love stories,' wrote Caryl Soriano of the New York Public Library for the always admiring *School Library Journal*.

Stephenie was often singled out for praise ahead of her co-authors.

'Meyer is didactic and original,' wrote Jenny Hale in the *Sun Herald*, although she concluded, 'A dark, light read – nothing that will stay in the mind.' This was an essentially fair point – these were short stories designed to divert the reader briefly. None was aimed at changing the world or making any lasting impacts. Short stories rarely do.

Stephenie is known to read – and be strongly affected by – the customer reviews left on the Amazon website about her books. She will have liked what she found on the page for *Prom Nights from Hell* – as would her fellow authors. 'This book is extremely clever and a great read. I got it simply because one of the five stories inside is by Stephenie Meyer, but I read all of them and came to realise that they are very original and fun!'

Another added, 'I recommend it. It's cool.'

The positive verdicts kept coming. 'Stephanie [sic] Meyer is on top form,' said another customer. 'This book was easy to get into and very enjoyable and I already know that it's one I will read again and again! Try it and see for yourself!!'

So thumbs up from the professional critics and the people Stephenie cares about even more – the ordinary, everyday reading public. It seems likely she will feel encouraged to return to the short-story form in the future. Perhaps she doesn't find brevity quite as testing as she fears.

Speaking of fears, her previous concerns over the whole prom experience were exorcised not just by writing the short story but also by the prom she arranged herself in May 2007. It took place at Arizona State University, which was established in 1885 and is based in Tempe. It was by no means a conventional prom night. For a start, the ratio of boys to girls was not the normal 50:50 but 10:1. On the night, the gym was decked with extravagant red and black decorations and Stephenie arrived wearing a fetching sequined burgundy wedding dress complete with rhinestones and beads. It was a truly *Twilight* event: models were hired to portray the parts of Edward and Jacob.

The idea for the evening came about when two 20-year-old *Twilight* fans from Long Beach, California, met Stephenie at a signing in the previous autumn. Christina Echeverria and Kady Weatherford told the author that they were planning to drive to her next signing in Arizona and were also thinking of dressing up and throwing a prom in honour of her visit. 'We said, "Let's have a party and wear pretty dresses,"' said Echeverria.

Stephenie was all for the idea. 'My publicist and I are girly girls,' she said.

She asked the two fans to form a prom committee, and announced details of the event on her own website. Tickets sold out in a day, so a second night was quickly added. It was easy for Stephenie to travel to the event, as by this time Pancho had given up work to look after the children.

Fans arrived in numbers over a thousand – with one *Twilight* fanatic coming all the way from London. They also flocked from all over America. 'I used all my Christmas money on this,' said 17-year-old Kristen Disabella of Flower Mound, Texas. 'I've been looking forward to this.' She added of her love of the *Twilight* story, 'I like the characters . . . It's hard to believe they're not real people.'

Another Kristen – Kristen Brabrook from Sterling – agreed and said she could relate to the characters because they're normal, not 'extremes' such as goody-goody cheerleaders or morose social outcasts. She and best friend Roni Baloy, 19, also of Sterling, flew in for the prom because they're 'passionate about things we love', Brabrook said. 'To be in a place surrounded by people who have the exact same passions you do, that's nice. Plus, you get to meet the author.'

As for the author, she was thrilled by the whole affair – in terms of confidence and enjoyment levels, she had come a long way since the days that she was physically sick with nerves in preparation for a promotional event. 'Everyone was gorgeous!' she recalled with a smile. 'The creativity and glamour blew me away.' She took to the stage to spectacular cheering and read the first chapter of the forthcoming *Eclipse* to the assembled 'Twihards'. She realised this was going to be a lengthy experience, and one that took a toll on her voice. 'There was lots of excited cheering, and I inferred from all the happy smiles in view that I was the only person in the room at that exact moment in time who was abjectly terrified,' she said. She was more comfortable signing books for the fans, and did so many of them that she ended up with a blister. 'I signed books until I had an actual blister on my index finger, which has never happened to me before,' she said. 'Then I had a chance to sneak over after the books were all signed and get my official prom picture.' That was taken with the models who on the night had played the parts of Edward and Jacob.

The models did a fine job on the night. However, the exciting news was soon to break that real live actors were going to be playing the parts themselves soon – on the big screen. First, though, there was the small matter of the next instalment of the *Twilight* story on the printed page.

Eclipse was published on 7 August 2007, with an initial print run of 1 million copies. The cover this time featured a torn red ribbon, set against the customary black background. This is believed to symbolise the feeling that Bella has of being torn between Edward and Jacob, and on a wider scale between the vampire and werewolf clans. The book marks a decision point for the heroine, as Stephenie explained, 'In both *Twilight* and *New Moon*, Bella commits to becoming a vampire without once really examining what price she'll pay. In *Eclipse*, Bella fully comprehends that price. And then she chooses to pay it. Every aspect of the novel revolves around this point, every backstory, every relationship, every moment of action.'

Any doubts or fears that her popularity had peaked were assuaged when it sold 150,000 copies in its first 24 hours on the shelves. In fact, it immediately made its presence felt in the bookseller charts when it knocked JK Rowling's *Harry Potter and the Deathly Hallows* from the top spot. Fighting stuff from Stephenie, who has been dubbed the next JK Rowling. The book trade had expected a fuss, but not on this scale. 'We were anticipating the book would be very big, but it has exceeded our expectations,' says Steve Riggio, chief executive of Barnes & Noble, America's largest book retailer. 'As booksellers, we're thrilled.'

Stephenie was thrilled too, naturally – and not a little relieved. The success of the book had been threatened when, due to a computer error, an online bookstore accidentally sent some copies of *Eclipse* out early to customers who had preordered it online. With the *Twilight* fanbase being such a Web-savvy crowd, there were fears that spoilers of the plot of *Eclipse* would spread like wildfire online. Stephenie and her publisher were afraid that the incident would turn into an echo of what happened with the publication of the seventh book in the *Harry Potter* series. Then, leaked copies were scanned and placed online page by page ahead of publication. Others were being sold on an Internet auction site ahead of official publication time. To avoid Web speculation about the plot, many online *Twilight* forums were closed down and Stephenie locked the comments facility on her MySpace page to avoid fans posting spoilers there.

It had been a scary experience for the author and publisher, and it had an unwelcome echo when it came to publication time for the special edition of *Eclipse*. The edition was to include the cover art and opening chapter for *Breaking Dawn*, making it a highly exciting and prized item to own. It was not due for release until the end of May 2008, but, again, copies were released early, rather ruining the drama of the official release. 'There's a lot of speculation on the Internet about possible covers, content and text of *Breaking Dawn*,' said Stephenie. 'I hope everybody knows that you shouldn't believe everything you see on the Internet. The only way you will know what is real is when you have the book in your hands. Until then, people should really take everything they see with a grain of salt.'

The fact that these incidents prompted such concern is extraordinary. Stephenie-mania is not to be underestimated and all details are game to be pored over and discussed. One is reminded of the famous maxim of the British football manager Bill Shankly, who, discussing whether football was a matter of life or death, quipped on a 1981 talk show, 'It's more important than that.'

The fans' passion is shared nowhere more strongly than with Stephenie herself, which is why she stands firm about many details of her story during the editing process. Her confidence has truly built since the days of the *Twilight* editing, when she remained largely quiet and compliant despite the unease she felt over the process. During the discussions over the *Eclipse* manuscript, she had been encouraged by her editor to include a sex scene in the story. She refused and was – she was pleased to say – supported in her stand by many of her young readers. 'It's a really good sign that children want to be children and adults want to be children again and experience that first kiss,' she said, heartened by the support and what it represented among her readership. 'I wish more of them didn't feel pressure to have sex. I know sex sells but I think romance does, too, especially if you do something well, and there is obviously a need out there for more books like this.'

For many, Stephenie's proof that you can make a success without resorting to sexual titillation is heartwarming indeed.

She had again been influenced by music in writing the book, she said. 'The most solid example of songs on the playlists being the ones that shaped the book was when I was working on *Eclipse*. I was in the car with my sister listening to "Hysteria" by Muse – we were out of town and I had my *Absolution* CD because I don't travel without it. We were listening to

"Hysteria" and the kiss scene between Bella and Jacob choreographed itself in my mind, down to the number of steps. I can hear him in the beat as he's walking toward her. The scene is not everybody's favourite, but I certainly enjoy it.'

As we shall see, the premise for her first adult novel was also prompted during a car journey. Her fans will hope she keeps dreaming and keeps driving, since both seem to be fertile ground for her imagination. Just don't try to do both at the same time, Stephenie.

The reviews that greeted the publication of *Eclipse* were mostly positive, though some focused in on Stephenie's use of adverbs. Rowling could have related to that – when her *Harry Potter* books were written up, the critics were often quick to be disparaging about her use of adverbs too.

If you wanted proof of the importance of Stephenie's books in the public eye, then you had to look not only at the content of some of the reviews but also the length. The prestigious *New York Times* newspaper's review was in excess of a thousand words. If Stephenie subscribes to the belief that one should not read one's own publicity, but weigh it, she will have felt satisfied. Lisel Schillinger, the *New York Times* reviewer, concluded with praise for Stephenie, and awareness of her unique situation: 'What subversive creature could dream up a universe in which vampires and werewolves put marriage ahead of carnage on their to-do lists?' asked Schillinger. 'The answer, of course, is a writer of steamy occult romantic thrillers who happens to be a wholesome Mormon mother of three – a category of one, solely occupied by Stephenie Meyer. The author is well aware of the jarring contradiction between her real and imaginary lives.'

The kids loved it too. '*Eclipse* by Stephenie Meyer is the best book I have read this summer,' wrote an admiring Megan Aurin in the *Pittsburgh Post-Gazette*, 'topping the last *Harry Potter* book. It is filled with more drama, more action and even more humor than the last two books by the author. I was riveted by the fast pacing, the turn of events and the always surprising outcomes. I would highly recommend this book to all of my family and friends. In reading *Eclipse*, I cannot wait for *Breaking Dawn*, the fourth book in Meyer's addictive series of Bella, Edward, Jacob and the rest of the engaging and identifiable characters.'

Marissa Dever, aged 12, agreed: 'I think *Eclipse* is one of the best books ever . . . It is EXTREMELY well written.'

With Stephenie maintaining the tradition of vampire stories working on the printed page, it was time for her stories to be tested out on the big screen. Life would never be the same again.

The journey from conception to publication for *Twilight* had been blissfully simple for Stephenie. The same story's transference from the page to the cinema was not quite as straightforward. She had been beyond excited when she sold the film rights to *Twilight* to the MTV/Maverick partnership in 2004 as she waited for the novel to hit the shelves. With Paramount Pictures lined up to make the movie, it was an exciting development for Stephenie.

She tried to keep her feet on the ground, though. Addressing a public event, she spoke with realism about her prospects. 'I know that they are on their second script revision, so they seem to be fairly serious about making it into a movie – although only about 20 per cent of books that studios buy the rights to actually make it to the screen.'

Her caution was merited: the plan hit the buffers when the time allotted to MTV in the deal ran out in 2007. Within months of this, changes were afoot at Maverick, too. The reported reasons for the fact that this deal never led to a *Twilight* film have been put down as script issues. Rumours suggest that the movie version deviated dramatically from the story on the page, including the presence of night-vision goggles and with Bella a different character from the one in the novel.

'They could have put that movie out, called it something else, and no one would have known it was *Twilight*,' she said. For month after agonising month, the idea sat in what is known in the industry as 'development hell' – meaning it had been bought by a film studio but was not being made. 'That was a horrifying experience,' says Stephenie. 'I had realised it could go wrong and that they could do it badly, but, when they did something that had nothing at all to do with the story, it was shocking to me because I'm really naïve.'

In the wake of that deal collapsing, Stephenie and her agency agreed – with a little reluctance on the part of Stephenie – to speak to other production companies to see if they could resurrect the deal. When word got round the industry that *Twilight* – by now a huge hit in the publishing world – was looking for a new screen deal, a number of companies raced to try to secure the rights. The company that landed the signature was Summit Entertainment.

Formed in the 1990s, Summit Entertainment is based near Los Angeles and was delighted to get the *Twilight* deal. Stephenie admits she was 'weary' following the Maverick debacle. 'The option period was up,' she recalls, 'and that's where Summit came in and said, "Can we roll over your option? Can we have it?"'

They had to work hard to persuade her to sign up with them, because she was still concerned by the way that the original filmmakers had planned to change the story for the big screen.

Erik Feig, president of production at Summit, did his best to reassure her that his company would stay true to her story. Among the promises he made were that 'no vampire character will be depicted with canine or incisor teeth longer or more pronounced than may be found in human beings'. She also insisted that there be 'no coffins . . . the characters have to exist by their present names and in their present forms, and they can't kill off anyone who doesn't die in the book'. She was not to be satisfied with vague, oral promises given in meetings: she wanted something firmer than that. 'I got it in writing,' she said. Here, the relative youth of the company was to her advantage, she felt. 'That's the best thing about working with a new company – they're really open to working with you.'

Stephenie signed and the news quickly created a buzz round the movie industry – her book was finally going to hit the big screen. The Twihards of the world were delighted.

Screenwriter Melissa Rosenberg remembers those days well. She said, 'When [Stephenie] went to Summit and they convinced her to let them option it, she insisted on a series of things . . . things that could not be changed. For instance, the characters had to be the same, the vampires had to have the same skills and same limitations. We had this manifesto we started with that was a couple of pages long. They sent it to me and I thought there was absolutely nothing on that manifesto that would hamper me. We've all had favourite books adapted for the screen then say, "Why did they do that?"'

Rosenberg adds that Summit used the size of the *Twilight* fanbase to try to tempt her into taking on the script, but it was not that fact that swung the decision for her. Instead, it was something closer to Stephenie's heart that helped her to make up her own mind. 'It was the characters that compelled me to take the job,' she said in words that would be music to Stephenie's ears. 'And actually, more than that, it was what Stephenie did with the vampire genre, which is one of the most well-trodden genres we have. She reinvented the mythology in a fresh way, and that's really quite a feat. I'm a big fan of the genre.'

The talent hired to direct the film was Catherine Hardwicke. As a child, says Hardwicke, she 'wasn't even really aware of cinema'. She grew up in southern Texas, close to the border with Mexico. It was an unconventional upbringing for Hardwicke, but that suited her. 'Since I was five years old, I knew that I was not ever going to have kids myself. Or ever smoke. Or drink. Or get married. And I never changed my mind.'

Her parents grew cannabis and she was always intrepid in her own childhood pranks. 'We'd sneak into Mexico and get shot at,' she said. 'It was really the Wild West.'

After leaving education, she was initially an architect but soon tired of that as a profession. She found it stifling and uninspiring. So she took a film degree and worked hard to break into that industry. Her first big success as a director was with the gritty film *Thirteen*. That film increased her standing in the movie world, as an unconventional yet talented act. 'I'm a weirdo, I guess,' she says of her reputation.

Weirdo or not, she was quickly considered just the person to direct *Twilight*. It was back in January 2007 that she bought her copy of the novel and sat down to read it. She recalls vividly the first time she read – or 'devoured' – the novel and how impressed she was by it. 'When I started reading the book, *Twilight*, I just got swept away into the feeling of this whole, almost obsessive love,' she said of the story she would take from the page to the big screen. She quickly identified the key themes of the story: 'delirious, obsessive, hypnotic, profound love'. She felt 'swept away' by the story, as so many readers did. '[Bella is] a really cool teenager, just falling madly in love, so in love with this guy that she would actually turn into a vampire to be with him . . . Stephenie really caught the spirit of being a teenager and of your first love.'

Nowadays Hardwicke still has the first copy of *Twilight* that she bought, but now it is packed with scores of Post-it notes, the text is heavily underlined and annotated and the whole mass of it is well worn and well read. Stephenie, a voracious reader, could relate, as could her character Bella, who wears out the books she reads in the *Twilight* story.

Stephenie was just as enthusiastic about Hardwicke as directing talent – and a person. '[She's] fantastic,' the author says. 'The first time we started talking to each other, I was surprised because I knew she was the person whose focus was going to shape this film. And so, if she had a different idea from me, it wasn't going to turn out like how I had seen it in my head. But we were on the same page from the very beginning, and she was already on top of the thing that I was worried about . . . So she was great because she got it in the same way I got it. I just really loved working with her.'

Their relationship has now moved beyond the professional, reveals Stephenie. 'We're kind of buddies. She's really cool to hang out with and she's just an awesome person.'

With this partnership so strong from the first meeting, Stephenie was increasingly optimistic about the chances of this film really working and accurately encompassing her vision.

All the same, Hardwicke felt a lot of pressure on her. In casting the film, she felt she had a major challenge on her hands because, as Stephenie admitted, she already had in mind actors she could imagine in many of the key parts. 'What's funny about this is, when I was writing *Twilight* just for myself, I was not thinking of it as a book,' says Stephenie. 'I was not thinking about publishing; yet at the same time I was casting it in my head because, when I read books, I see them very visually. I pretty much cast every book I read. I'm thinking, "Who could play this? Who would do this?" I did exactly the same thing when I was writing *Twilight*.'

She had earlier confessed that – in her imagination at least – she had already cast real actors in several of the parts. 'I have certain actors who would be my first choices for certain roles, including Henry Cavill for Edward, Emily Browning for Bella, Charlie Hunnam for Carlisle, Rachel Leigh Cook for Alice, Graham Greene for Billy, Cillian Murphy for James, Daniel Cudmore for Emmett.'

No wonder Hardwicke felt such a high degree of pressure on her as she approached the actual casting for the film. 'The first challenge for me was to find the perfect Bella,' she recalled, aware of what a brilliant character she was. 'Stephenie created a seventeen-year-old with quiet courage – but a capacity for profound love.'

Hardwicke soon had somebody in mind for the part. 'I had seen Kristen Stewart's brief but powerful performance in *Into the Wild* and I was impressed with her depth and vulnerability. When she is sitting on the bed in the trailer, her intense yearning and desire was palpable.'

Born on 9 April 1990, Stewart was raised in the heart of the American movie industry – Los Angeles. Her father is a television producer and her mother works in script supervision. At the age of 12, she had her first big part in the superb blockbuster thriller *Panic Room*, starring alongside Jodie Foster. By the time she came under Hardwicke's gaze, she was filming the comedy drama *Adventureland* in Pittsburgh. The director flew overnight to meet Stewart there and, despite the fact that the young actress had been filming all night, she showed herself to be an instant professional. 'She learned her lines on the spot,' Hardwicke says of Stewart's impressive approach on the Sunday, her day off. 'She danced on the bed and chased pigeons in the park. I was captivated.'

The director flew back to Los Angeles and reviewed the footage of Stewart's acting. She knew straight away that she had found her Bella. With this role filled, it was time to cast the role of Bella's obsession – Edward Cullen. This was a key decision: who could convincingly carry off this part and ignite in the hearts of millions of teenage girls the obsessive lust that Bella feels for him in the book? She and the casting directors considered thousands of actors for the part. She personally met dozens of young men, but all too often they did not fit the part.

'They mostly felt like they were the boy-next-door, not an other-worldly vampire,' she recalled in *Twilight: Director's Notebook*. She admits she got worried, and felt under enormous pressure to deliver 'the perfect Edward'. Among those to audition was an actor called Michael Welch, who was considered wrong for the part of Edward but was given the part of Mike Newton. Still, though, the crew were no closer to their perfect Edward.

Another actor who auditioned for the role was Dustin Milligan, star of *90210*, a spin-off of *Beverly Hills 90210*. 'Unfortunately, I didn't have a British accent, so I didn't get the job,' he quipped. This was a reference to Stephenie's preference that an English actor take the part of Edward Cullen. Her first choice for the part had been British actor Henry Cavill, star of *The Tudors*.

'Indisputably the most difficult character to cast, Edward is also the one that I'm most passionately decided upon,' she wrote on her website. 'The only actor I've ever seen who I think could come close to pulling off Edward Cullen is Henry Cavill. Henry was Albert, the young son in *The Count of Monte Cristo*. Can you see it? I know I can!'

The problem was that, at 25 years of age, Cavill was going to struggle to fill the part of a 17-year-old character who does not age throughout the four-part story. 'The ravages of time have taken their toll,' joked Cavill.

Stephenie was not happy to see him discounted. 'The most disappointing thing for me is losing my perfect Edward,' she wrote. She proposed that he be given another part in the film – that of the head of the Cullen family, Carlisle Cullen, although he was not given that part either.

Still the filmmakers had nobody for the part of Edward Cullen. Cometh the hour, cometh the (young) man. Robert Pattinson had just appeared in a film called *Little Ashes*, and his agent was keen to get him back on the big screen, striking while the iron was hot. Born in London in 1986, he was best known for his part in two of the *Harry Potter* series of films. With his undoubted pin-up looks, he quickly became a hot prospect in film. As the *Twilight* filmmakers were looking for an Edward, Pattinson's agent sent him along to some casting auditions and one of those was for *Twilight*. He had filmed his own audition tape, so keen was he to get the part. This was a method that had worked for other actors of his generation: Elijah Wood did the same when going for the part of Frodo in *The Lord of the Rings* trilogy. So Robert and a male friend filmed the scene that takes place in a chemistry class. However, he was too embarrassed to send the footage in. After all, the scene is supposed to take place between a male and female character. He felt the same when he auditioned. 'I was literally embarrassed walking into the audition,' he said. 'I thought that even going into the audition was completely pointless, because they were just going to cast a model or something. I felt it was kind of arrogant of me to even go in. I was almost having a full-on panic attack before I went to the screen test.' He took some of the antidepressant drug Valium to try to calm himself down.

However, he had no reason to be so anxious because Hardwicke was impressed with his audition, though she admits she had not always been convinced. 'I didn't think of him initially,' says Hardwicke. 'I was really desperate, and he looked OK in that movie, but that was a while ago and I never imagined him to be the right person. But we had it down to four choices, and he was one of them.'

Along with the others on the shortlist, Pattinson flew to Los Angeles for the final auditions. At night he slept on his agent's sofa; by day he auditioned. 'He flew over on his own dime to LA, slept on his agent's couch, and we had finals at my house,' recalls Hardwicke. 'The four guys came over and they read three different scenes with Kristen. When we got to Robert and Kristen, we did the kissing scene on my bed. And I watched it and I thought, OK, these two have the chemistry, they have the sparks, you feel the intensity, and the passion. And I knew at that moment that we could make a good movie.'

It had been an unlikely route to the 'finals' for Pattinson. 'This was just a way-out choice,' she said. 'I'd seen *Harry Potter and the Goblet of Fire*, but I hadn't met him. It was getting down to the wire and I was, like, "Who is this guy?" and it was kind of dodgy on the phone as we were trying to figure each other out.'

With Pattinson awarded the part of Cullen, the two lead characters were cast. For Pattinson this prompted a period of further anxiety as he got his head around how to play the character Stephenie had created in the book. 'I basically spent two months thinking, OK, how can I play this character like he is written and be absolutely nothing like him in real life?' he told *Vanity Fair*. 'How can I get away from the most major aspect of his description – his appearance?'

He felt the way that Stephenie had written the book

made his challenge harder in the cinematic version. 'As it is written from Bella's perspective, she describes him in this obsessively lustful way. She does not see a single flaw in him at all . . . So it took me ages to think of it, but it ended up being really simple: if you are in love with someone, you can't see any flaws in the other person. So I finally figured out that I didn't have to play the most beautiful man on the planet, but just play a man in love.'

This was not the first time he had been cast to play a character described as astonishingly attractive in a novel. He played the Cedric Diggory character in the *Harry Potter* franchise. Diggory is a student two years above Potter in the school's Hufflepuff house. He is described in Rowling's books as 'absurdly handsome'. Pattinson admits that playing such a part can be offputting.

Pattinson enjoyed reading *Twilight* and the other novels in the series, but naturally found this a strange experience too, knowing he was to portray the hero on the big screen in front of millions. 'Not in their entirety before getting the script, no. I did my screen test, had the weekend before my next meeting for it, and read all three over one weekend. I obviously really liked them, but it is always strange reading a book knowing that I am hopefully going to play the part. It's read in a very different context.'

He feared that the book was vulnerable to a 'cheesy' cinematic treatment. 'I just thought the whole thing was going to be really silly,' he said, 'but [Kristen] really shocked me when I went in to audition.'

Pattinson was not Stephenie's personal first choice, but she was pleased to learn he had the part. 'I am ecstatic with Summit's choice for Edward,' she announced. 'There are very few actors who can look both dangerous and beautiful at the same time, and even fewer who I can picture in my head as Edward. Robert Pattinson is going to be amazing.'

Not that she had been aware of who he was initially. 'They told me that they have got this guy and he's interesting. So I Googled him and I thought, OK, this could work. Then I saw him in costume and he was the Edward I saw in my mind.'

However, she is honest about how she felt immediately after discovering his casting. 'When I found out that Robert Pattinson was given Edward's role, it was a terrible moment for me,' remembered Stephenie. 'Edward existed in my head; he had a face, a smile. I was really sceptical. But when I saw him I was immediately conquered. I can understand why girls are so attracted to him. Robert Pattinson has done a terrific and impressive job. He is exactly how I imagined Edward.'

Stephenie's first meetings with the cast were surreal to say the least – heated, too, on occasion. 'Before the filming started I'd just come in and meet everyone,' she recalled. 'With Rob we sat down and talked about Edward's character. It wasn't an argument, but we actually disagreed on his character. I said, "No, this is how it is." He said, "No, it's definitely this way." And the funny part about it is that we are arguing about a fictional character, yet in the performance he did what he wanted and it was exactly what I wanted. So that was really cool.'

She was blown away by him as a personality. 'He's a very mesmerizing person to be around,' she said. 'He's got such a compelling personality.'

Pattinson is a pin-up to girls across the globe – could Stephenie ever imagine dating him? 'I don't think you'd want him for a boyfriend,' she said. 'And you couldn't just be his friend because he's terribly sexy!'

Just as Stephenie was impressed with Pattinson, he was just as pleased by the choice of his opposite star Stewart. 'When I met Kristen,' he said, 'there was instant chemistry. She brought something out of me that I can't even explain.'

With filming under way, she saw the cast in costume. 'It was really surreal,' she recalled. 'The first night I was on set, I went to dinner and it was the first time I had met any of the cast. They came straight in from a photo shoot, so they were in costume. And there is nothing in the world like sitting down at a table with a bunch of people who are people you made up. It was just bizarre. And they looked amazing. I don't think I ate the whole time I was there, because I was so keyed up and nervous.'

Once the casting process was complete, producer Greg Mooradian said that the thoughts of the passionate fanbase that had built up around Stephenie's novels were considered during the casting process. 'On the fan websites, every single person who'd read the book had already cast the film for you twenty times over. We did take a look at their ideas and we decided we were never going to please everybody, so what we had to do was go with our guts. The actors we cast are the actors we feel best embodied these characters. It took forever to cast this movie, but, once we found Bella and all of the Cullens, I realised we finally had it. When I actually got to see them together performing in a scene, it took my breath away.'

Indeed, recalls Mooradian, he had experienced a similarly overpowering reaction when he first read the *Twilight* book. That reading actually happened, as is often the case for his first glance at novels that may be suitable for cinematic treatment, prior, even, to the book's publication. 'Part of my job as a producer is to scour the world for new material,' he recalled. 'When this one came across my desk, I just couldn't put it down. The premise of a girl falling in love with a vampire just hit me like a ton of bricks. And the book delivered on every level.'

He expanded on his assessment of *Twilight*, and how he had his work hat on as he pored over its pages. 'There is no way to predict the life of a book,' he said. 'You have to go with your instinct. Often, when I'm reading a young-adult book, I have to imagine whether a fifteen-year-old girl might enjoy reading it. What struck me in my initial reading of the *Twilight* manuscript was how much I enjoyed it, how completely absorbing it was, even while knowing I was far afield of who the book was supposed to speak to. My reaction told me this was more than a book for a young girl.

'This was a first-time author's unedited novel, but I was able to see past [its raw quality] because the themes of the story and characters were so wonderful. It had universal themes, like *Romeo and Juliet*, which certainly influenced this book. It struck me this was a great movie premise – it seemed the greatest idea nobody had ever done. But at the time there was no way to predict it would connect with every young girl in America the way it has, that it would become an anthem for young girls as much as anything in contemporary culture.'

Stephenie, too, felt the book always had a strong cinematic feel to it. 'When I was writing the novel I saw it as a movie. It was a very visual experience so I really wanted to see it brought to life.'

So as it began to be brought to life, did the assembled cast embody her vision? 'Yes,' she confirmed. 'If someone had pulled me in there and said, "We've got a roomful of your characters – let's see if you can pin their names on them," it would have been so easy. They were so clearly who they were. I think the acting in this movie is something special. It's amazing. A lot of these kids are new and they're so good.'

Stephenie may have been pleased, but not all were

initially. Far from it, in fact. When news of the cast broke, the *Twilight* fanbase made their feelings plain. Much of their passionately delivered opinion centred on the casting of Robert Pattinson in the Edward Cullen role. Quickly, an online petition was started by fans who were opposed to this choice. It quickly gathered more than 75,000 signatures. One online wag commented that he was the wrong choice because he resembled a gargoyle. He learned of all this opposition via his mother, who had searched the Web for any mention of him and emailed him links to all the pages. It must have been upsetting for him to learn of all this, but, in truth, for every fan who opposed his casting another was avidly in favour of it. He was taken aback by the power of the *Twilight* fans. 'It just baffles me,' he said. 'It's nice, though.'

Hardwicke remembers well the reaction: 'People were sending emails: "He's revolting! He's disgusting! He can't be Edward!"'

Stephenie's views on the ongoing work were never expressed that way, but, all the same, there were inevitably moments of tension between author and filmmaker during the process. 'All of us have seen books ruined as movies and I had a lot of things I wanted to protect. My stipulations were very basic: "You can't kill anyone who doesn't die in the book. The Cullens have to exist by their right names and in their right characters." Things like that. I wanted the groundwork to be there.'

With the work under way, the only time Stephenie really put her foot down was during the casting process. She was insistent that Kellan Lutz be cast in the role of Emmett. 'My personality is such that I have a really hard time being critical with other people,' she says. 'I can be critical of myself all day long. But I hate to step in and say, "I really wish this was different." But it's been good for me in general to have to speak up because I am so invested in this. I've forced myself, like with the Emmett situation, to take a step forward and say, "I don't like this." That's hard for me, but I'm glad of every time I did it and I don't think I stepped on too many toes and everyone seems to still like me.'

As the film was being made, the army of *Twilight* fans were following proceedings as closely as they could. The whole process was being dissected before the film was even released. Here was proof positive of the pressure that all involved were under. The *Twilight* fanbase would not accept anything but the best from the screen version. Some of them even tried to get a part in the film themselves. The Make-A-Wish Foundation is a charity that makes young people's dreams come true. It is used to seeing those dreams revolve around established acts, but, while the film was still in production, it was receiving *Twilight* movie-themed requests. Among these were requests from *Twilight* fans for parts in the film, as extras. 'You can't make this up,' said Hardwicke.

The part of Jacob went to Taylor Lautner. He

admitted he had not heard of the *Twilight* story when he first considered the role. 'Yeah, this one's kind of big,' his agent told him. Lautner replied, 'I've never heard of it.' When he learned it was based on a book, he asked how big the book was. 'So I check it out and it's just mind blowing,' he says of the popularity of Stephenie's novel. He was suddenly nervous, realising the pressure and excitement there would be around the part. 'Oh my gosh!' he said to himself. 'What am I getting myself into? This is life-changing!'

As he scoured the Internet and realised the sheer scale and passion of the *Twilight* fanbase, he became absolutely determined to land the part – and was thrilled to do so. He felt it would be a hit on the big screen, where its appeal would be broader than it was on the printed page. 'What we tried to do with the film is add a little more action and horror to it. So now it's for everyone,' he said.

Although top billing went to Pattinson's and Stewart's characters, for Stephenie the part of Jacob is very important indeed. She has become increasingly fond of him. 'Jacob is an ordinary kid who has to deal with extraordinary things that he wasn't prepared for. I love Jacob. Because he's such a sixteen-year-old boy. I just love him as a character. He's become such a bigger part of the story because I had such a soft spot for him. I have been surrounded by boys, with my kids, my brothers, my father and uncles, so he was very familiar to write about.'

For many Twihards, the two males – Edward and Jacob – are rivals. Many fans have polarised into two groups: Team Edward and Team Jacob. However, for Stephenie there is plenty in common between the two. 'Jacob and Edward are similar in that they both want to be good people. They try their hardest to do their best, to do everything that's important to them.'

Another of the cast – though one who took a very small role – was Stephenie herself. She agreed to take a cameo role in the film and was given the part of a character in a diner. She had needed to be convinced. 'It was not my idea to do the cameo,' she said. 'They talked me into it. They thought it would be, you know, cute for the fans because most of them would recognise me. I was thinking it was going to be more like a "Where's Waldo?" thing. Like I walk by for one second in a crowd and, if they can find me, cool. That's the one scene in the movie I would happily cut – the first five seconds, and the one that I had to watch, like, I mean, like this [covering her eyes], "Ah, is it over yet?" It was really hard for me.'

She was originally going to have a speaking role, in the form of her ordering a vegetarian dish. Stephenie feared, though, that this might be a step too far and risk distracting from the film itself. Instead, then, she was merely served the dish without speaking. 'How horrible would it be if there was this moment where I'm so horrible and it just takes everybody out of the moment, and all of the suspended disbelief is gone, and everyone's like, "Wow, she sucked!"?' she said.

There are plentiful precedents for authors appearing on the big screen during adaptations of their books. For instance, American literary legend Saul Bellow played the part of Man in the Hallway in the adaptation of his novel *Seize the Day*, and more recently Michael Chabon appears in the big-screen version of his first novel, *The Mysteries of Pittsburgh*.

There are also several examples of authors appearing in movies generally. Writer, poet and wit Dorothy Parker appeared in *Saboteur* as far back as the 1940s; Gore Vidal can be spotted in *Gattaca*; horror giant Stephen King is in several movies, including *Maximum Overdrive*; and Truman Capote can be glimpsed in New York's Central Park in Woody Allen's fantastic comedy *Annie Hall*. As for Salman Rushdie, he has made more than one cameo in a film, popping up in *Bridget Jones's Diary* and *Then She Found Me*.

As well as asking the filmmakers for a change to be made to her own scene, Stephenie also asked for one of the most crucial scenes in the film to be reshot. The kissing scene between Edward and Bella is key not just in the *Twilight* narrative, but that of the entire four-part saga. When she saw the footage of the scene, Stephenie felt the kissing was too full on. Not only did this run against her preference for the *Twilight* story to be restrained in its sexual aspects, but she also felt it was too soon in the saga for such intensity. 'The problem is, if you're going to continue with other movies,' she said, 'there's a very gradual build to their physical relationship'.

Once the film was complete – or wrapped, in movie-speak – it was time to sit back and await the reaction of the critics and viewing public. 'These books have every element of a totally satisfying blockbuster,' said publisher Megan Tingley. How right she proved to be!

Yet one of the earliest responses to it from the media was negative – bizarrely so. 'It's probably not any good,' wrote online film critic Josh Tyler. 'In fact, it looks like a direct-to-DVD castoff, but its fans are so addicted to the books that they are lining up to see it in droves. In fact, the thing is already selling out . . . The Twekkies will be out to see this thing in force on Friday. The question is: will anyone else? The trailers look terrible and I don't know anyone who hasn't read the books who's even remotely interested in seeing it.'

He must be eating his words to this day. A more optimistic prediction was made by journalist Moira Macdonald, writing in the *Seattle Times*. 'Meyer, despite her occasional penchant for purple prose, vividly creates a world of gothic, edge-of-danger romance, the kind in which bookish girls have long loved to lose themselves on rainy afternoons . . . For the movie it would appear that the Titanic audience is already in place: according to a Movietickets.com poll of about 2,000 moviegoers, three out of four females said they planned to attend *Twilight* on its opening weekend, as well as 77 per cent of those polled who were under 25 . . . But if the film catches enough of Meyer's brooding romance and breathless suspense . . . there might just be long lines at the multiplexes for a while. Because preteen and teenage girls – and at times their grown-up counterparts – like to revisit favourite stories, over and over again.'

So there was plenty of cause for optimism and excitement on the evening of the premiere in Hollywood on 17 November 2008. Stephenie wore an ankle-length black-and-white dress on the evening. She caused every bit as much excitement as the cast did when she walked up the red carpet and smiled for the photographers. She was in jubilant mood. 'I don't think any other author has had a more positive experience with the makers of her movie adaptation than I have had,' she said. Praising the performances of the cast, she singled out Pattinson for winning over the Twihards who had so doubted his casting. 'I think everybody warmed up pretty fast,' she said. 'Some of it's that British thing, his charmingness, and some of it's that he's drop-dead gorgeous.'

With the premiere and associated festivities done, it was time for the film to open to the general public. Some had predicted it would flop; some were convinced it would soar. Which prediction would be proved right on the night?

The queues at the cinemas on the opening weekend were long indeed. It opened with a series of special midnight showings, which had been sold out far in advance. During the opening weekend alone the film grossed over $70 million, more than double the sum it cost to make. Movie industry analysts were surprised by this figure. The consensus had been that it would reach $60 million at the absolute most, because it appealed primarily to female viewers. However, it had exceeded their wildest expectations. The day after it opened, Summit Entertainment announced that it planned to bring the *Twilight* sequel, *New Moon*, to the big screen too. All in all, then, a triumphant weekend for Stephenie.

This time, the views of the critics would not directly impact on her. After all, the film was someone else's work. All the same, she followed them with interest. Manohla Dargis, writing in the *New York Times*, was in two minds about the film. 'It's love at first look instead of first bite in *Twilight*, a deeply sincere, outright goofy vampires romance for the hot-not-to-trot abstinence set . . . This carefully faithful adaptation traces the sighs and whispers, the shy glances and furious glances of two unlikely teenage lovers who fall into each other's pale, pale arms amid swirling hormones, raging instincts, high-school dramas and oh-so-confusing dramas.'

Entertainment Weekly's Owen Gleiberman was particularly cutting from Stephenie's point of view. He said, 'What Hardwicke can't quite triumph over is the book's lacklustre plot. On screen, *Twilight* is repetitive and a tad sodden, too prosaic to really soar. But Hardwicke stirs this teen pulp to a pleasing simmer.'

The *Washington Times* concluded, 'It's hard not to get sucked in – if one can get past the sometimes hokey, melodramatic teenage dialogue. This is first in a long string of *Twilight* movies . . . and intriguing questions remain.'

In the UK, the response was often more upbeat, particularly from Stephenie's perspective. Sukhdev Sandhu, writing in the *Daily Telegraph*, was approving of the film and the way it captured the old-fashioned restraint of Stephenie's book. 'I watched *Twilight* in a cinema full of young girls who, when they weren't texting friends and guzzling soft drinks, giggled, sighed and exhaled with a passion that was not only endearing, but a measure of its emotional truth.'

Sandhu was not the only person to watch the film in a packed cinema. After a strong opening weekend, the fans kept on coming. Richie Fay, president of domestic distribution for Summit, said, 'This certainly exceeded our expectations by a great deal. The fanbase was huge.'

With the book on the big screen, Stephenie had to get used to a dramatic increase in *Twilight* mania. So too did her cast. Pattinson happened to be in a DVD store the day the film was released on that format. He was amazed to see people queuing up to buy it, some in tears. His 23rd birthday was besieged by fans. He is grateful to them and he felt that the excitement of the *Twilight* fans exceeded that of another novel-cum-film. 'There is this strange kind of connection that some people have to the books,' he said of Stephenie's work. 'It can be pretty extreme. I think there are fans of *Harry Potter* . . . that are like that as well, but I guess this story is just so intimate that people think they really know the characters and can feel the emotion.'

In preparation for greeting thousands of screaming fans at premieres and other events, Pattinson dresses accordingly. 'I always find myself wearing a lot of layers as well so they can't see you hyperventilating – that's a good preparation technique,' he told the BBC. For now, he says, he is comfortable enough with the fame that Stephenie's novel has brought him via the film. 'There's always places you can disappear to. It just involves a little bit more thought. You can't just wander around willy-nilly,' he says. 'It's such a novelty to me still. If I'm still stuck in hotel rooms in ten years and I haven't figured out any other way than hiding, it probably would annoy me a little bit.'

Acquiring his *Twilight*-earned superstardom had proved to be a rollercoaster experience for the actor. After auditioning on Valium, he got the part, but, as we've seen, his casting was immediately opposed by many fans and even initially disappointed Stephenie. She was quickly won round, though, and the fans soon followed – but not before the aforementioned backlash, an occurrence that Stephenie said 'broke my heart'. She was truly concerned about the effect the fuss had on Pattinson, showing a degree of personal responsibility that was very high. 'Because I've had my tiny bit of celebrity, I'm aware of how hurtful those things can be,' she said. 'I apologised to him for ruining his life. He said his mom was sending him links like, "Oh no, they called you a gargoyle." They just raked him over the coals. The way he took it was a lot more positive than the way I would've handled it. He was like, "I'm going to prove them wrong. I'm going to go out there and prove them wrong."'

With the first novel in the *Twilight* saga successfully on the big screen and further adaptations to come, it was time for a new novel from Stephenie. This time it had nothing to do with Bella, Edward and vampire romance. If anyone thought that this author's talent and appeal were one-dimensional, they were about to be proved wrong.

chapter six
the hostess

As we have seen, when she was a child, Stephenie Meyer would liven up long family car journeys by telling stories to her parents and siblings. As an adult, she was also struck by a key scene for the *Twilight* series while behind the wheel. The long tortuous hours on the freeways of America proved a fertile ground for her imagination back then. In her adult life this has not changed at all. She still finds that car journeys can provide great inspiration and it was one such experience that fuelled the story that took her from the *young*-adult shelves onto the adult shelves for the first time.

Twilight came to Stephenie in her sleep, but the concept for *The Host* came to her when she was wide awake and driving through the Arizona desert. 'The kernel of thought that became *The Host* was inspired

173

by absolute boredom,' she recalls. 'I was driving from Phoenix to Salt Lake City, through some of the most dreary and repetitive desert in the world. It's a drive I've made many times, and one of the ways I keep from going insane is by telling myself stories.'

Her children were sitting in the back, watching a film on the in-car DVD player. Here she stayed true to a hobby she began as a child during those long family drives to visit the grandparents in Utah. She would make up stories in her head and speak them out loud to the family. She has not changed in this regard, but this one was about to turn into something more than a quickly forgotten, journey-based caper.

So that was the physical location for the inspiration, but, as to where it came from within her psyche, Stephenie is rather more flummoxed. 'I have no idea what sparked the strange foundation of a body-snatching alien in love with the host's body-boyfriend,' she confesses. 'I could tell there was something compelling in the idea of such a complicated triangle.'

Having been thus inspired during the desert journey, she grabbed a notebook and sketched out a basic plot outline for the story. She uses a cinematic metaphor to explain how the inspiration process comes about and moves onwards. 'Well, it's like you get this kernel of the story, with some really great points that could go many different ways,' she says. 'It's like the explosion of a kernel of popcorn. You've got this little thing with so much potential . . . and it expands in front of you.'

Expands is the operative word, for the story she was about to write would eventually weigh in at more than 600 pages. Some of those who read it would complain that this was too long, and the story told too slowly.

Just as with *Twilight*, she was keen to get to work as soon as she could. Ever fearful of the onset of poor memory that sometimes arrives as the years flow by, she followed the formula of many successful authors – the moment you are struck by inspiration make sure you get the idea down on paper the best you can. She scribbled down as much as she had in her head, and awaited the chance to get back to her computer. Then she started to put together the story proper. At this stage, this was meant to be just a side project that she could work on for her own personal amusement, as a distraction from the editing process she was stuck in on the *Twilight* series. 'But it turned into something I couldn't step away from until it was done,' she says.

'*The Host* is just a story I had fun telling myself. My personal entertainment is always the key to why a story gets finished. I never think about another audience besides myself while I'm writing; that can wait for the editing stage.'

Those who wish to become the next Stephenie Meyer should gather round and note this recurring theme in her *modus operandi*: write for yourself and enjoy the process most of all. 'If you love to write, then write,' she has advised. 'Don't let your goal be having a novel published: let your goal be enjoying stories.'

So how would she sum up this new story she wrote? 'It is science fiction for people who don't like science fiction,' she said of *The Host*. She very much dislikes providing a synopsis for a story she has written. She admits that brevity is not her strongest point. However, she had a go at summing up *The Host* story for MTV.

'Basically, the easiest way for people to get it in a nutshell is that it's *Invasion of the Body Snatchers*, if the aliens had won,' she said. 'That gives you a sense of the horror, but these body snatchers are so kind and so good, and the world is such a good place when they're in charge, it makes it hard to hold their colonising against them. Then there's the main [story] – that people don't give up even after [their bodies] have been given away as a host – and there are two entities with one body to share between them.'

The book begins with the poem 'Question' by May Swenson as an epigraph. Swenson (1913–89) was an American poet and playwright who, like Stephenie, grew up in a Mormon household. Unlike Stephenie's, though, her work moves beyond the boundaries of Mormon-induced primness and is frequently erotic, with lesbian themes. 'Question', however, asks how one would survive without one's own body – a highly relevant theme for the story to come.

And that story kicks off with the reader being introduced to Melanie Stryder, who is the human body in which the invading soul resides. Stephenie says that the fact the heroine's name almost rhymes with her own is merely coincidence. 'No, that wasn't on purpose,' she says. 'With names, for human characters that aren't a hundred years old, I tend to look for people around me. Melanie is one of my cousins, and Stryder is actually someone I knew in high school.'

Melanie and the invading soul have quite an adventure during the story, which has been a new experience for Stephenie to compile: new characters, new target readers and a new plot. In writing *The Host*, the biggest challenge for Stephenie was the constant internal dialogue between Wanderer, the soul, and Melanie, the host body. Dialogue can be a challenging task for any author. In setting such a premise for *The Host*, had Stephenie made her job much more difficult here? Not so, she says.

'Wanderer and Melanie were very distinct personalities to me from day one; keeping them separate was never an issue. Melanie is the victim – she's the one that we, as humans, should identify with; at the same time, she is not always the more admirable character. She can be angry and violent and ruthless. Wanderer is the attacker, the thief. She is not like us, not even a member of our species. However, she is someone that I, at least, wish I was more like. She's a better person than Melanie in a lot of ways, and yet a weaker person. The differences between the two main characters are the whole point of the story. If they weren't so distinct, there would have been no reason to write it.'

It sounds easy when she puts it like that, but one suspects most people would find it a far more challenging experience. That was not the only aspect of the story that confused some observers. What, many could not help but wonder, did Stephenie mean when she gave *The Host* the surprising description of 'science fiction for people who do not like science fiction'? 'Reading *The Host* doesn't feel like reading science fiction,' explained the author. 'The world is familiar, the body you as the narrator are moving around inside of is familiar, the emotions on the faces of the people around you are familiar. It's very much set in this world, with just a few key differences. If it weren't for the fact that alien stories are by definition science fiction, I wouldn't classify it in that genre.'

She added that there were a few thematic similarities between *The Host* and the *Twilight* series, but essentially they stood apart. 'The only thing that's similar is my style and focus. It's about the people. It's not about the alien invasion or the science fiction, really. It's about the people, and that's the same way the other books aren't about the horror or the vampires: they're just about people. But, really, nothing else. It's a whole different world.'

Some people quickly drew comparisons between *The Host* and Philip Pullman's *Northern Lights* (named *The Golden Compass* in the USA and filmed under that name). Asked whether her story was along the same lines as *The Golden Compass*, Stephenie was insistent it was not. 'It really isn't. I did read *The Golden Compass* . . . recently and it's really fascinating. But this is really different. This is aliens – and, once they're in, the people are out. So it's not that same symbiotic relationship.'

However, Lev Grossman drew a parallel between *The Host* and the *Twilight* series in his *Time* magazine profile of Stephenie. 'Like *Twilight*, *The Host* is a kinky setup – two girls in one body! – played absolutely clean,' he wrote.

Although *Twilight* was aimed very much primarily at young-adult readership, it ended up being devoured by adult readers too. *The Host*, too, crossed over, but in the reverse direction – from its core adult audience to young adults. Stephenie had never expected any different.

'I've had a great deal of interest from my YA [young adult] readers about the release of *The Host*,' she said at publication time. 'I have no doubt that they will continue to make up a core part of my readership. I love blurring the lines between the different genres and categories, because, in my head, a good book won't fit inside the lines. I hope that *The Host* continues to do what the *Twilight* saga is doing: showing that a good story doesn't belong to any one demographic.'

As ever, Stephenie was very much focused on and attached to the characters of her stories, and discussed them at the time of publication. 'The two main characters who are, you know, sharing a body have things I want to be and things I wish I weren't . . . You have Melanie, who's really, really strong physically – and I wish I could be like her because she can do anything. Nothing stops her. She's really, really strong emotionally, so she can handle anything. But she also can be really mean. Whereas Wanderer, the other personality, is totally compassionate, absolutely cannot hurt another person, and is just as kind as I would wish I could be. But she's weak, too . . . And so they both have things that I want and things that I wish I didn't have.'

With Bella in *Twilight*, Stephenie had wished she could have had her as a friend; with Melanie she wanted to be her, and Wanderer too.

So what was this entire story about, if anything? Was there an overall theme or message? As she told *Vogue* magazine, the subtext to the story for her was about that most 21st century of preoccupations: body image. It appears this is something she has grappled with, but also something she has put more into perspective as a result of writing *The Host*.

'I'm not critical of others, but I am very critical of myself,' she says. 'When I was working on this, I had to imagine what a gift it is to just have a body, and really love it, and that was good for me, I think.'

Another angle she enjoyed exploring as she wrote *The Host* was that of love. 'Getting to explore love from so many different angles' appealed to her, she said. 'Love for community, for self, for family –

romantic love and platonic love.' She later added, 'One of the things that I find really enjoyable to explore is the idea of love. I like looking at my own life and my friends and family and how love changes who you are. It fascinates me.'

She was optimistic that it would appeal to the reading public, including the Meyer fanbase, despite its differences from her previous works. 'It's definitely a departure in that it's a whole new cast and crew in my head,' she said. 'I think my established readers will be comfortable with it; they'll get into the rhythm of it and find it sounds like me.'

The manuscript had gone up for auction among different publishers, and, naturally, there was a fierce scramble for it. She eventually sold it to Sphere for $600,000. The initial print run was for half a million copies – reflecting the confidence that the publisher had in the novel. The confidence was justified. The online bookstore Amazon named it one of its books of the month for May, a supremely influential endorsement for online sales. It stood alongside the likes of *Nixonland* by Rick Perlstein, *A Case of Exploding Mangoes* by Mohammed Hanif and *Beijing Coma* by Ma Jian. The accompanying text was naturally very admiring of the book. '*The Host* is unabashedly romantic, and the characters (human and alien) genuinely endearing. Readers intrigued by this familiar-but-alien world will gleefully note that the story's end leaves the door open for a sequel – or another series.'

The write-ups were – as is often the case with her work – a mixed bunch. Carol Memmott reviewed the book for the influential *USA Today* newspaper. '*The Host* is *The X-Files* meets *Days of Our Lives*,' she said. 'Despite some sticky-sweet dialogue, Meyer's story and characters will stoke fans of both sci-fi and romance. Unlike the classic human-vs-alien stories in which ghastly looking creatures (think *Alien*) are the norm, Meyer offers aliens so docile you wonder how they managed to take over the earth. Still, the effect is frightening.'

Jeff Giles in *Entertainment Weekly* felt that the book had its good parts, particularly towards the end. 'As in her *Twilight* series, Meyer is more interested in relationships than in flashy genre conventions,' wrote Giles. After losing its way and moving at too slow a pace, he believed, it picked up again towards the end. '*The Host* starts rolling again in its last hundred pages and Meyer's affirmative life lesson is disarming. If only the rest of the book had as much soul.'

Olivera Baumgartner-Jackson was initially perturbed by the book. It seemed too long, she said, and the premise of the story as outlined on the back cover seemed uninspiring. However, the reviewer's conclusion for *Bookwatch* was music to Stephenie's ears. 'Stephenie Meyer's *The Host* is a proof that one should never judge the book by its cover, especially not by its back cover. If I would have let myself be turned away by the outline of the story as it appeared there, I would have missed an incredibly entertaining, thought-provoking and fascinating read. As for the 600+ pages, all I have to say at this moment is that I hope the sequel – and I sure hope there is one! – will be at least this long.'

Praise indeed, though the *Las Vegas Review Journal* was less enthusiastic. '*The Host* is told in Meyer's distinctive style – first-person narration in extreme detail, lazily telling a story where the main conflict isn't even hinted at until several hundred pages have passed. I just wish she could have waited until after she finished the *Twilight* series to write it. *The Host* is an enjoyable read, a page-turner that, like all of Meyer's books, lacks a classic plot and villain. The main conflict of the story isn't really introduced until the reader is 500 pages into the more than 600-page book.'

Time magazine's Lev Grossman provided a rich and essentially glowing assessment in his extensive profile of Stephenie. 'Like Meyer's other books, *The Host* is about love and choice and demi-human creatures. ("I rarely write about just humans," Meyer says. "You can get humans anywhere.") *The Host* is also set on the same slow burn as Meyer's other work: while there's hot kissing, it's a strict PG. But *The Host* is a grittier read – much of the book is set in a hardscrabble resistance hideout. Nobody has nice clothes. There's romance, but much of *The Host* is about Wanda's [Wanderer becomes known as Wanda later in the story] attempts to fit in with her new human bedfellows, about feeling alone and different and unlovable – literally alienated. If there's a formula to Meyer's work, it holds true here: she rewrites stock horror plots as love stories, and in doing so, she makes them new again.'

How would the online community respond? Blogcritics.org's Lisa Damian cheered from the rooftops in her write-up of *The Host* – and then some. 'By number-one *New York Times* bestselling author Stephenie Meyer, [it] is a riveting page-turner that was nearly impossible to put down. It is the kind of book that keeps me up reading late into the night, and when I turned the final 619th page, I still wished for more.'

Praise indeed, and she had not finished her love-in with Stephenie's first adult novel. Damian seemed almost embarrassed by her own enthusiasm for *The Host*. 'I rarely offer such effusive praise in a book review without some accompanying critical observations, but the fact of the matter is that when I consider my favorite books of 2008 thus far, *The Host* is at the top of my list.'

Ruel S De Vera of the *Philippine Daily Inquirer* agreed that the book crossed over from an adult readership to embrace a younger one, too. 'It is literally the best of two worlds, and Meyer proves her *Twilight* success is no fluke,' said De Vera, who came to a rousing conclusion that Stephenie must have enjoyed immensely. 'If you liked Stephenie Meyer's work before, you will adore *The Host*, a worthy new work from a creator who not only defies expectations but is also navigating her own undiscovered way, echoing the realization Wanderer makes: "Nothing like me had ever existed before."'

The reviews were important to Stephenie, who makes no secret of her interest in them. Some authors claim never to read any of the critics' judgements, which seems unlikely in some cases. Stephenie, though, does read them.

In the United Kingdom, the reception was less glowing in some quarters than it had been in America. The *Guardian*'s Keith Brooke was measured in his verdict. '*The Host* veers too often into either melodrama or sheer tedium . . .' he wrote. 'When it's good, the novel works well, and will appeal to fans of the author's hugely bestselling *Twilight* series, but it is little more than a half-decent doorstep-sized chunk of light entertainment.'

Lisa Tuttle, writing in *The Times*, was rather disparaging. 'The aliens are depicted as so passive and easily fooled that their conquest of the Earth is hard to credit, and I found the author's view of adult relationships easily the creepiest aspect of this novel take on *Invasion of the Body Snatchers*,' she tutted.

Beth Taylor of Wales's national daily the *Western Mail* could hardly disagree more. Taylor described *The Host* as 'a gripping read that makes important comments on love, friendship and human nature'.

The *Derby Evening Telegraph* reviewer came to *The*

Host fresh, in the sense that the critic had yet to read any of Meyer's previous work. 'What is striking about it is that it is rather laboriously written,' he concluded. 'Meyer never uses one short sentence when a detailed explanation over two pages will do, which makes the book rather heavy going and somewhat easier to put down than pick up. It's a weighty tome at more than 600 pages, so it needs to be faster-paced than this if it is to keep this reader's attention. It has had a lot of rave reviews, but I was left wondering if some or even many of them came from people who already loved her earlier work. Coming to *The Host* cold, as someone who doesn't especially enjoy science fiction, I found it rather ludicrous in premise (obviously) and frankly not engaging enough to draw me into the other world that the author has created.'

Happily, the *Daily Mail* gave the book the thumbs-up, saying, 'She may still be best known for the angst-filled *Twilight* series about lovelorn teenage vampires, but this year Meyer published her first book for adults. Giving that reliable sci-fi standby – body snatchers – a distinctly emotional twist, she wonders what would happen to the world in the aftermath of a successful invasion by alien parasites. What follows is a highly unusual love triangle.'

The capital's (now defunct) freesheet *London Lite* was also mightily impressed. 'Not original, but the twist is that alien Wanderer can't help listening to the thoughts of Melanie, whose body she inhabits, falling in love with Jared, the man Melanie obsesses over,' wrote Lauren Paxman. 'The (female) reader can't help falling for Jared, either. Scarily addictive.'

So that was the critical response to *The Host*. On a broader level, Stephenie was truly ruling the book trade in both America and the United Kingdom. The UK book industry's trade magazine the *Bookseller* documented this trend soon after the release of *The Host*. 'Publishers and retailers have a lot to thank Stephenie Meyer for,' it purred. 'So far this year, just shy of 15m [pounds sterling] has been spent on her novels in the UK this year. By the half-way point almost 10p in every £1 spent on a children's book went towards a copy of one of the four books that comprise her *Twilight* series – five editions of which make the top six below, along with her adult vampire thriller, *The Host*.'

Down under in Australia, the reviewer for the nation's edition of the *Daily Telegraph* was sceptical of the premise for *The Host* but felt that some fresh twists were important. 'The tired concept of aliens landing on Earth undetected and slowly taking over the physical shapes of human beings gets a re-run in this thriller,' wrote Lucy Chesterton. 'What saves it from being yet another version of *Invasion of the Body Snatchers* is a darkly different premise. What if the alien takeover turns this planet into a better place than it was when humans were in control? Love interests between humans, whose bodies have been taken over, and those who have not add to the tension.'

Chesterton's compatriot Terry Oberg reviewed the book for the *Courier Mail* and took a similar approach. 'It's a deliciously horrifying concept, used countless times to the point of becoming a tired cliché,' he wrote, 'but Meyer takes it one step further. What if the invaders won, and changed the world irrevocably and arguably for the better? And what if the few scattered survivors of humanity witnessed this new utopia and were confronted with the fact that, perhaps, they didn't deserve the planet in the first place?' Oberg concluded, '*The Host* is the best kind of science fiction – full of thought-provoking ideas and imaginative concepts, and free of technobabble and cardboard characters. [Meyer's] first adult novel has been highly anticipated, and it won't disappoint.'

It's a love triangle that will soon be seen on the big screen, for in September 2009 the screen rights for *The Host* were snapped up by producers Nick Wechsler and Steve and Paula Mae Schwartz. Stephenie had not been short of approaches from other movie figures for the rights, but had turned down all pitches up until this point. A variety of aspects of this approach conspired to swing her in its favour. She was impressed, she says, by 'a significant offer, a strong vision for the project, and a collaborative spirit'.

It also helped enormously that Andrew Niccol was on board to write the script. Niccol had recently worked on *Gattaca* and *The Truman Show*, which are two of Stephenie's favourite science-fiction films, both residing in her top five sci-fi flicks list. The deal was done, and *The Host* was headed for the cinema.

As *Cinematical* magazine observed, this development would cement her status as queen of the geeky circuit. 'Get prepared, Con geeks,' wrote Monika Bartyzel. 'If this does even half as well as *Twilight*, you can bet your bottom dollar that her presence at Comic Cons [fan conventions] will continue to grow. I mean, she's got vampires and aliens – she's just one technopunk or wizard away from full-on geek love.'

Once more, we can note here the unlikely place Stephenie as a woman has on the cultural map. There are precedents for female writers who have penned stories about vampires, most notably Anne Rice. However, for Stephenie to be such a key figure in the geeky and therefore highly male world of science fiction is a definite oddity. Female voices are rare in that world and particularly so at the large conventions that are such a central part of the social life of the geeky army. For Stephenie, she has had to adjust to speaking at such events and now largely enjoys, rather than endures, them.

She also enjoys and feels more confident with her involvement in the filmmaking process. For *The Host*, this was a fact that was welcomed. 'We wanted Stephenie to be involved in the adaptation and have her endorse and be part of the creative decisions,' Wechsler said. *Twilight* has 'proven she knows more about what works than most'.

She was keen for the adaptation of *Twilight* that the cast be up-and-coming actors, but for *The Host* she feels they can look higher up the celebrity tree. 'With *The Host*, I think the actors could be really big names. That would be cool. I'd love to see Robert Redford put on a beard and be Jeb; he would be amazing . . . Matt Damon has some very Jared-esque qualities. And then [I'd love to see] Casey Affleck as Ian and Ben Affleck as Kyle. Imagine the interplay.'

Asked whose body she would like to invade, as ever the geeky and fun Stephenie was willing to play along with the concept. 'I'd really like having a couple of days of being a rock star, although I'd rather be a backup – like maybe the drummer for Muse,' she said. 'It would also be fun to be gorgeous, like be Charlize Theron, just for a couple of days.'

She has also authorised a skateboard company called Hobo Skate Co. to produce a line of *Host*-related merchandise. It included T-shirts and skateboards, and the ever-generous Stephenie ensured that charities benefited from the hook-up. 'We are stoked to have Stephenie on board with Hobo,' Hobo founder Jared Hancock said. 'Her global popularity and worldwide success gives us a huge boost in selling products that will contribute to our cause. A portion of all sales will go to the Hobo Foundation that helps homeless families who have been forced to live on the streets.'

Stephenie has also supported other charitable causes, including Project Book Babe. In April 2009 in Tempe, she auctioned valuable items including: lunch with Meyer, Meyer's red beaded dress from the local *Eclipse* prom party, autographed manuscripts of *Eclipse* and *The Host*, complete with inked comments from Stephenie and her editor. Project Book Babe is to benefit Stephenie's friend – and book-trade figure – Faith Hochhalter. She was closely involved in the design of the merchandise range, ever the hands-on character.

'We created an image of *The Host* exactly as Stephenie Meyer pictured it in her mind,' Hancock said, with his co-founder Chad Swenson adding, 'Stephenie has been fantastic to work with. Her extraordinary talent and imagination behind *The Host* gives us incredible design concepts to work with. Even with Stephenie's insane schedule with *New Moon* and *Eclipse* movie productions, she has worked with us on every detail to make sure the products are remarkable.'

With *The Host* very much hitting the mark, she could afford to be increasingly confident and pleased with herself. People were loving the book, and the prospects for the film seem huge. Perhaps the most satisfying moment of praise she received for *The Host* came from a friend, who told Stephenie, 'I'm so proud of you! Because we're not sure if JK Rowling is a one-hit wonder. But you're not!'

That conversation took place during the busy promotional tour for *The Host*. When she came back

191

home from that tour, Stephenie found that she had just three days to make her final tweaks to the concluding novel of the *Twilight* series – *Breaking Dawn*. She worked from 6 a.m. until midnight to get it perfected. This was the book that would – for the time being at least – close the saga. Nothing could be allowed to spoil it – including the sort of online leaks that rather tainted the release of *Eclipse*.

To try to stave off any leaks, Stephenie took control of the situation in the run-up to the publication of *Breaking Dawn*. She allowed *Entertainment Weekly* magazine to run an extract from the book in May 2008. Then, in July and throughout August, she published on her website a 'quote of the day' from the novel. She also issued a plea to her fans – via her website – not to help distribute any leaks that might occur. 'As we saw with *Eclipse* (not to mention that last *Harry Potter* book), there is always the potential for copies of the book to be leaked early,' she wrote. 'My publisher is doing everything they can to prevent this, but there is only so much that can be done. This is the favour: if someone, somewhere, somehow, gets a copy early, I'm asking you to please not post any spoilers on the internet. And if you see something, please don't spread it around.' Her democratic, engaging style with her fans gave Stephenie enormous clout. Many listened to her pleas, leak or no leak.

The excitement around the world of *Twilight* fans was tangible. 'Stephenie Meyer has written a dazzling grand finale to an epic love story,' said her publisher Megan Tingley as the book prepared to hit the shelves. 'And, with the extraordinary excitement surrounding the publication of *Breaking Dawn*, I'm thrilled that legions of new readers will now discover the saga that has already captivated millions around the world.'

This time the cover featured a chessboard. In the background was a red pawn, in the foreground a white queen. '[It] is a metaphor for Bella's progression throughout the entire saga,' explained Stephenie. 'She began as the weakest (at least physically, when compared to vampires and werewolves) player on the board: the pawn. She ended as the strongest: the queen. In the end, it's Bella that brings about the win for the Cullens.'

Breaking Dawn was published on 2 August 2008. It was scheduled for release at one minute past midnight and there were parties across the world to greet its publication. The imaginative bashes were defined by *Twilight* saga themes: lookalike contests, trivia quizzes, hunting games, face and fang painting and the like. The Godiva chocolate company even created a limited-edition *Twilight*-themed chocolate bar to mark the occasion. 'The *Harry Potter* phenomenon created something of an event release around books. What we found with *Harry Potter* is the same that we found with *Breaking Dawn*,' says Trevor Dayton, vice-president of kids and entertainment for the Indigo book chain. '[Readers] don't just want to walk into the store on a Saturday afternoon that it's available, pick it up and go home. They want to make a moment of it and celebrate it.'

In Britain, there was just as much excitement, with 400 copies being sold in just 20 minutes at the Borders shop on Oxford Street in London. The expectation of a big demand had led to an initial print run of 3.2 million copies, with another 0.5 million added at the last moment. It sold 1.3 million copies globally in its first 24 hours on the shelves, which is the most a Little, Brown book had ever sold on the opening day on the shelves. (The figure is given some context when you consider that the hit author Dan Brown sold just 1 million in the first day that his much-hyped novel *The Lost Symbol* was on sale.) So, good news in terms of sales, but in terms of reception Stephenie would need to prepare herself for quite a lot of controversy.

The reviews started favourably enough. *Time* magazine gave it an A-rating and said, 'After three volumes of slow-motion foreplay, the last novel in the mega-best-selling *Twilight* series finally tells us everything we always wanted to know about sex (and marriage) with vampires but were terrified to ask. It's a wild but satisfying finish to the ballad of Bella and Edward.'

The *School Library Journal*'s write-up concluded, 'While this novel is darker and more mature than the earlier titles, Meyer's twists and turns are not out of character. Fans . . . will flock to it and enjoy it.'

Mary Harris Russell, in the *Chicago Tribune*, wrote, 'Meyer continues to produce witty writing about families, teenagers and popular culture . . . *Breaking Dawn* is a fun read.'

It was *Publishers' Weekly* that first put the boot in, feeling that the plot for *Breaking Dawn* was implausible and convoluted. 'Essentially, everyone gets everything they want, even if their desires necessitate an about-face in characterization or the messy introduction of some back story.'

Entertainment Weekly gave it a D-rating and predicted that readers who had loved the first three instalments would 'lose all patience with the franchise midway through *Breaking Dawn*, when Meyer takes her supernatural love story several bizarre steps too far'.

The *Washington Post* was even stronger, saying that 'the ick factor goes through the roof in *Breaking Dawn*, which is, frankly, dreadful'. Reviewer Elizabeth Hand continued, 'It gets worse: *Breaking Dawn* has a childbirth sequence that may promote lifelong abstinence in sensitive types . . . Reader, I hurled.' It concluded, 'The most devoted readers will no doubt try to make excuses for this botched novel, but Meyer has put a stake through the heart of her own beloved creation.'

Not all the fans were devoted enough to eschew criticism. Complaints had already been made by fans when they read the advance-released opening chapter.

Stephenie tried to look on the funny side of this. 'There were a lot of people,' she chuckled, 'who said, "This isn't the real first chapter, the writing is so bad!"'

There was also disappointment that the story had ended at all, though for Stephenie this was a no-brainer. 'The Twilight Saga is really Bella's story, and this was the natural place for her story to wind up,' she wrote on her website. 'She overcame the major obstacles in her path and fought her way to the place she wanted to be. I suppose I could try to prolong her story unnaturally, but it wouldn't be interesting enough to keep me writing. Stories need conflict, and the conflicts that are Bella-centric are resolved.'

She listened to the controversy but, still, she was the author, and it was up to her when the story ended. All the same, she related to the passion: 'It's inevitable that the bigger your audience gets, the bigger the group who doesn't like what they're reading will be. Because no book is a good book for everyone. Every individual has their own personal taste and experience, and that's why there are such a great variety of books on the shelves. There are lots of very popular books that I don't enjoy at all. Conversely, there are books that I adore that no one else seems to care about. The surprise to me is that so many people do like my books. I wrote them for a very specific audience of one, and so there was no guarantee that any other person on the planet besides me would enjoy them.'

Occasionally, though, criticism stings Stephenie

hard. Never in her career had she faced as much as she did with the publication of *Breaking Dawn*. It hurt and she admitted it. 'It's a bit hard for me: I'm very thin-skinned. I used to read all the reviews on Amazon.com. I could read 100 five-star glowing reviews and the one review that's one-star – "This is trash" – that's the one that sticks with me.'

Some fans even went as far as returning their books to the stores. A spokeswoman for her publisher weighed in with her support. 'With a book as eagerly anticipated as *Breaking Dawn*, there's going to be diverse reactions,' said Little, Brown's Melanie Chang. 'Stephenie Meyer's fans are incredibly passionate about her books, so it's no surprise that readers respond with equal passion.'

There were also happier notes when *Newsweek* magazine praised the fact that the cross-generational appeal of her books was helping to increase mother–daughter bonding. The sensitive way that Edward and Bella remain abstinent before marriage has helped some mothers approach the awkward discussion of the facts of life.

For Stephenie, though, the pain of the experience was tough. The book's sales, on a positive note, were exceeding her expectations – but so was the level of criticism. 'It's been hard,' she said. 'The book did so much better than I thought it would . . . And then the negative reaction was so much more than I was expecting.'

Fans formed a 'Team Stephenie' to help defend her and she received many heartwarming notes of encouragement from around the world. She met many of the fans face to face at promotional events. At one such occasion, a fan asked her, ahead of reading *Breaking Dawn*, whether the story would feel complete at the end of it. Stephenie answered, 'I can't really answer that question for you, but I felt closure.' In any case, the book contained her favourite moment between Bella and Edward, which came in the final two pages of the work. 'I mean, they finally see eye to eye and really know each other,' she smiled. 'And, wow, that was really worth two thousand pages to get to.' She also enjoyed the moment in which the Edward–Jacob rivalry is finally put aside, admitting she cried while typing that passage.

The irony of the controversy is that *Breaking Dawn* nearly never existed. She had originally planned for the *Twilight* saga to take place over just three books. However, she decided that she wanted to give the story one more outing. 'When you create a world like that – when you create Edward and Bella – if you stop writing, it's like you're killing them,' she reasoned. 'I couldn't do that. I had to let them go on and see what was going to happen.'

Another irony is that, having refused to 'sex up' scenes in *Eclipse*, Stephenie was asked to tone down some of the passages in *Breaking Dawn*. They felt the violence was too explicit and asked her to soften the relevant scenes. There was even a time in which they considered giving the book an age rating. 'It was for an age limit of fifteen or sixteen and a warning,' Stephenie revealed of the conversation. 'I think the content is just a little harder to handle, a little bit more grown-up for really young kids. I have nine-year-old readers, and I think it's too old for them. Some of it's violence, and some of it's just mature themes.'

Some had loved *Breaking Dawn*, some had – in all honesty – hated it. For Stephenie the passion it evoked in people was tough at times. She could console herself, once the controversy had died down, when many of those who had responded unfavourably to the book changed their minds and spoke of how highly they regarded it. The book has received numerous awards. She won the WH Smith Children's Book of the Year for 2008 for the novel. It also won the Teen Choice Book of the Year for 2009 in the Children's Book Choice Awards.

For the promotional tour for *Breaking Dawn*, Stephenie took a different approach. Putting aside the traditional signings and readings, she put on a *Breaking Dawn* Concert Series tour instead. She visited four major US cities – Chicago, New York, Los Angles and Seattle – with Justin Furstenfeld of the rock band Blue October alongside her. 'Music played a major role in the writing of the *Twilight* saga and it's thrilling to be able to incorporate my love of music into these special events for my readers,' she beamed. 'I'm a huge

Blue October fan! To have Justin at these *Breaking Dawn* events playing songs that inspired scenes in the book is cooler than anything I could have imagined.'

Thousands of fans were lucky enough to attend the events in person, and those who could not get in were able to follow proceedings online. More than a quarter of a million people did just that.

Stephenie Meyer had managed to avoid any leaks of *Breaking Dawn*, as had happened with *Eclipse*, but she was about to face another leak that would really hurt her. It should have been Stephenie's happiest hour. She had successfully launched her four *Twilight* novels and *The Host*, too. Just months away was the premiere of the *Twilight* movie. However, she then learned that a work in progress of hers – *Midnight Sun*, a book that would tell the *Twilight* story from Edward's perspective – had been leaked and posted online. She was devastated and put a statement on her website: 'As some of you may have heard, my partial draft of *Midnight Sun* was illegally posted on the Internet and has since been virally distributed without my knowledge or permission or the knowledge or permission of my publisher.' After much soul-searching she had decided to reclaim control of the situation by placing the unfinished work on her own website, in order that fans could read it without having to feel they had been dishonest towards their favourite author.

'I'd rather my fans not read this version of

Midnight Sun,' she explained. 'It was only an incomplete draft; the writing is messy and flawed and full of mistakes. But how do I comment on this violation without driving more people to look for the illegal posting? It has taken me a while to decide how and if I could respond. But, to end the confusion, I've decided to make the draft available here. This way, my readers don't have to feel they have to make a sacrifice to stay honest.'

Alison Flood, writing in the *Guardian*, was not upset by the development. 'I can't say I'm all that disappointed: another take on the same story seems a little tedious to me,' she said. 'Wouldn't it be better to let it rest, revel in the phenomenal sales of the books, and move on to a new set of characters and a new storyline?'

Many of her huge global fanbase want to know where we are left with the *Midnight Sun* issue. Might we see a finished book published in the future? 'I don't know. I need to feel alone with something in order to write it, and I do not feel alone with that manuscript at this point. So many people chimed in on it. Everything that I've written except for six pages was leaked. It was an early draft; I'm over the shock of it, but I'm not over the feeling that everyone's involved with it. It doesn't feel like mine any more. But I'm hoping that with time . . . it's so clear in my head I'd like to go back to it. You don't need to worry that I'm not hearing this every day from my mother. She goes, "You know, Stephenie, maybe you should think about that one." She loves it, she wants it real bad. So I'm definitely getting the pressure, don't worry!'

So we may well not have heard the last of the *Twilight* series. We certainly haven't heard the last of Stephenie Meyer either. She has numerous new projects on the go, on the printed page, in the cinema and beyond.

This multitalented woman is bubbling with creativity and ideas.

chapter seven

mermaids
in malibu

Stephenie Meyer had been mad about music ever since her university years, when – free from the censorious clutches of her parents – she submerged herself into a sea of rock and pop tunes that became part of her life and have been so ever since. Among the bands whose music became the soundtrack to Stephenie's life was Jack's Mannequin. The four-piece band are a pop-rock outfit based in Los Angeles, though they originally hailed from Orange County. The band were formed in 2004 by lead singer Andrew McMahon as a side project – he was already the front man of a similar musically styled band named Something Corporate. Soon after Jack's Mannequin released their first album, called *Everything in Transit*, McMahon was diagnosed with leukaemia. He fought the disease hard and has since made a full recovery. His side-project band have since put together a second album called *The Glass Passenger*. The lead single from their second album was called 'The Resolution', released in August 2008. When it came to commissioning the production for the promotional video of the song, they turned to Stephenie, who was a publicly confirmed fan of the band and had imagined which of the characters in her novels would be their fans. 'She said part of her process in creating characters was finding out what music they like,' McMahon said after meeting her.

He explained how this all came about. 'It's kind of a funny story,' he said. 'Before I knew much about Stephenie or the *Twilight* series, a friend was on her website and found Jack's Mannequin on a playlist related to one of her early books. She told me about this and I was obviously flattered.'

For the time being, though, he did not think that this connection would be taken further creatively. It was not until they had a band meeting two months later that they struck on the idea. 'We looked for a video treatment, we didn't find anything that we particularly liked and ended up throwing out in this brainstorm session, "Why don't we reach out to Stephenie Meyer, who's written these huge books?" We did, and she was into it and that's how it got kicked off.'

He had not personally read the *Twilight* books, but began to once he got in touch with her – out of creative respect as much as anything. 'I couldn't get into a room and let the woman direct the video unless I'd taken in her art as well,' he admitted magnanimously. He swiftly realised just what a phenomena he was holding in his hands. 'I'm quickly becoming super-aware of how big of a deal it is,' he said once he had begun reading *Twilight*.

'It was sort of a pipe dream, I guess, in a sense,' said McMahon of the hopes that she would agree to get involved. But, like the *Twilight* story itself, it was a dream that came true. Stephenie had been utterly delighted to receive this invitation. 'She was real receptive,' enthused McMahon. 'She's awesome to work with,' he added, 'a very cool lady.'

It was a clever move by the band, as their connection with Stephenie guaranteed them plentiful column inches of publicity and garnered them the attention of a host of new teenagers, who follow everything Stephenie does with enthusiasm. 'Stephenie connects with millions of people, and that's pretty substantial,' McMahon said.

The very cool lady wrote two 'treatments' and the band were impressed enough to choose one of them to form the basis of the video. 'Treatment' is industry-speak for an outline that is prepared on paper for a music video. A treatment will include the basic concept of the video, a chronology of events or plot of the video and many other elements, including the location, the atmosphere, pace and any other salient details. The band will then examine the treatment. In Jack's Mannequin's case, they liked what they read.

Indeed, so impressed were they that they not only took the treatment, but invited Stephenie to direct the video as well. This was a huge deal for her, because this was entirely new territory. All the same, her intrepid side is always willing to consider new experiences, so she agreed to take on the task, but it was a big challenge for her – if an exciting one. 'I don't know much about directing,' she admitted. 'It's a total fluke. I'm just doing it because it's fun and an experience I never had, and I didn't want to turn it down. I certainly wouldn't say I'm going to be a music director now! I don't even know how to work the camera, and they won't let me. They don't want me to break things. I think "creative consultant" is a much better word [for what I'm doing]. I'm just making sure the vision looks right.'

McMahon and his bandmates were unconcerned with her lack of experience in the field, because they were convinced she had the correct instinctive know-how to make it work for them and their audience. 'She had never directed a video before, but she knows how to appeal to people's pop nature,' said McMahon.

The video itself is a fantastic affair. It begins with the sight of a heart, drawn into the sand on a beach. McMahon then begins to sing, outside a remote deserted seaside house. The action then returns to the beach, with a view of the ocean. Here we see the first hint of the mermaid character. As McMahon sings about clearing the wreckage from his past, the heart on the beach is destroyed when the tide washes over it. As he walks to his vehicle (an ancient Ford pickup, not unlike the red Chevy that Bella drives in the *Twilight* books) complete with suitcase in his hand, the sea begins to follow him. The lyric protests that, wherever he hides, she will find him regardless, he fears.

As he drives up a mountain, the water continues to follow him. 'It's sort of a fable,' Stephenie explained. 'This mermaid doesn't take no for an answer. The more he tries to get away from her, the greater lengths she goes to to be able to reach him, and so that ends up meaning a lot of water climbing things. He's running from the water. Even if he climbs a mountain, it still comes after him.'

McMahon sits at his piano, singing plaintively, 'And you hold me down,' as the tension of the narrative builds. From the top of the mountain he looks down on the beach through a telescope. Through it, he – and the viewers – can see the tail of the mermaid, dancing in the sea once more. In the video's closing section, he walks into the sea as the vocals repeat the word *resolution* over and over. He finds the mermaid, who is lying looking ghostlike, face up under the water, seemingly dead. As he reaches out his hand to touch her, she turns into a heart shape, the same one we earlier saw on the beach.

The video closes with a shot of McMahon's face,

which holds an expression that suggests that a resolution of sorts has occurred, if not an entirely happy one. 'To me, it references a relationship that was not healthy for one person, [but] that didn't matter to the other person,' Stephenie said. 'They still wanted what they wanted, and I thought this was an interesting way of interpreting that. It's really just normal relationship angst, and adding the supernatural element is just a way of making it a little more visual.' With typically witty understatement, she concluded, 'Because, really, a couple not getting along is not as visual as an ocean stalking a person.' There can be little argument about that, Stephenie.

The Jack's Mannequin vocalist was mightily impressed by her ocean-as-stalker concept. 'Ultimately it's rooted in the idea of running from something rather than facing it,' said McMahon of Stephenie's concept. 'It plays out visually with me packing up my piano and trekking inland, away from the beach, as the ocean is swallowing up the land. I won't give the ending away, but I will say there is a mermaid in the mix.'

Working on it was strangely enjoyable for the band, who insist that Stephenie's involvement coincided with a change from the normal slog-like experience. Instead, they reported, it was an enjoyable, if at times arduous, experience for the band and crew. 'It was a very cool shoot,' enthused McMahon of the filming, which took place in Los Angeles. 'Music videos are a tricky thing. They require a lot of trust in the team creating the visuals, and that can be a little scary. That said, there was a great vibe on the set, and shooting by the water really made it an especially peaceful day, despite all the hard work that goes into it.'

Stephenie loved working on the shoot, which took place at a beach in the luxurious surroundings of Malibu in California. As McMahon explains, although she had a directorial role she was not filling the role of director *per se*. 'It wasn't like she was behind the camera, you know – she's an author,' he said. 'There was this guy named Nobel Jones, who is a director, and she was on set the whole time. She obviously wrote the treatment, and she and Nobel collaborated quite a bit as far as the execution of her vision and how she wanted it to look. She was definitely there and approving shots and giving her opinion of certain shots as we went along, so she was definitely a part of the production and the directing of the video, sure.'

She was, for her part, self-effacing: 'Clearly, I have no experience. They're just running things by me.' All the same, she was directing things to a reasonable extent – and all this in the glamorous surroundings of Malibu, an extravagant and idyllic seaside area just outside Los Angeles, and down the road from the famous Venice Beach.

'It's all about what could you get to realistically in one day,' she said of the location in Point Mugu, 'so you have the sense of travelling without really travelling. That was the tricky part.' Midway through the shoot, Stephenie told an *LA Times* reporter, 'It looks good. It looks the way I imagined it, so that's really cool.'

McMahon and Stephenie were both pleased with the final outcome, which they felt was relevant – but also irrelevant – in all the right places. 'It's cool,' said McMahon. 'It's not some sort of exposé on my life . . . It's nice to know we're going to make a video for the sake of making a video. [We're] making something that's kind of fantastic and different and exciting but isn't about the song specifically, and it isn't about me specifically,' he buzzed.

He and Stephenie could not help but roll their eyes at the memory of the widespread assumption that her involvement would mean the video would be dominated by vampires and other fantasy creatures. 'The mermaid was as [fantastical] as we got,' said McMahon. 'She was even laughing about it – that everybody thinks we're going to shoot a vampire video.'

McMahon was delighted with the outcome of the collaboration and says he can pinpoint how the connection worked to such stunning effect. 'It works so well, because [with my music] I always try to create something super-visual and create a backdrop where people can take a bunch of experiences but relate them. And she's done that in a huge way with her books.'

Stephenie has not said a great deal publicly about the experience of working with the band, but McMahon is convinced that she enjoyed the experience. 'She seems genuinely enthusiastic about it,' he told MTV during the shooting. 'She's in the middle of editing her film right now, so I guess the implication is that she's excited because she's taking time away from her baby to make it. But, like I said, I'm most excited because, when I was making this album, I wanted to find someone who was really talented and get them to write a treatment and just leave it alone and let it fly. And that's exactly what we're doing here.'

He had never imagined a mermaid as having anything at all to do with the song, and he admits that some in his party were surprised to read that Stephenie wanted to include one. For him, though, it was details like that that sold him on her concept. 'What I loved about Stephenie's is that it was creative,' he said. 'I mean, I loved the metaphor, I loved that she made it more sort of this bizarre kind of love story. There's the water rising and representing the kind of love that you can't escape, sort of thing, and there's the mermaid at the end. The mermaid sort of freaked people out in the treatment, but I was like, "Let her do her thing. She obviously has done well enough for herself; I've got a crazy feeling it's going to be OK." And I think they nailed it. But was I writing about mermaids? Definitely not.'

Stephenie says she has always been fascinated by mermaids, and enjoyed including one in the video. 'When I was letting my imagination run wild for this, there were several different storylines I came up with and this one I thought had the most visual impact.' Might she write a novel involving mermaids in the near future? 'I don't know if I will or not,' she said.

The song was fairly successful commercially, reaching Number 27 on the Billboard Hot Modern Rock Tracks chart. Although Stephenie has just about ruled out directing more music videos, don't bet against her returning to the field one day. She loves music and did a great job with Jack's Mannequin. The right offer at the right time from the right band could get her very enthusiastic again. As for McMahon, he is keen to reverse the roles and write a song for a future movie adaptation of a Stephenie novel.

'Yeah, of course I would,' he said. 'But that's like one of the biggest trench wars in the entire music business, just people trying to get their artists on future *Twilight*s or things like that, you know. I tend to find, when it comes down to things like that, where it's just a bloody bath over everybody trying to force their way in the door and figure it out, that I tend to shy away from it. But I would love to have a song featured in *New Moon*, no question. I don't tend to write from a writing-assignment standpoint, I write what I feel in my day-to-day life, and if there's something from that that inspires the person putting the soundtrack together enough that they want to use it, then, God, of course I would be totally honoured, you know? Whether or not I'll go sit down and pen a song with *New Moon* in mind is maybe a different story.'

He missed the boat for *New Moon* but the rather tantalising prospect of Stephenie's working again with her musical hero McMahon seems fairly likely, so watch this space.

There was a lot of respect among critics for Stephenie's video for 'The Resolution'. The teenage website *4tnz!* was gushing in what it saw as a very appropriate link-up: 'The band's sort of emo. Edward Cullen's sort of emo. We think it's a good match!' The MTV television channel sent down location reporters to cover this historic cultural collaboration. The channel's website cheekily headlined its report '*Twilight* Author Stephenie Meyer Tries to Drown Jack's Mannequin in "Resolution" Video'.

Meanwhile, as the *LA Times* confirmed, Stephenie's involvement increased the appeal of the song to a new audience. 'The Meyer connection seems to be giving the song some extra lift, married, as it is, to the author's enormously successful book series and an overlapping romance-inclined youth audience,' wrote the newspaper's 'Soundboard blog' author, Susan Carpenter.

At the end of 2008, tributes continued to be paid to Stephenie and her work. In its Person of the Year awards, *Time* magazine named her as one of its 'People Who Mattered'. 'Maybe Americans aren't ready for a Mormon presidential nominee yet,' said the entry, with a nod to the growing popularity of mixed-race presidential nominee and future President Barack

Obama. 'But they're more than ready to anoint a Mormon as the best-selling novelist of the year.'

Writer Lev Grossman concluded the entry, 'Sometimes nice girls do finish first.'

Sometimes they do indeed. Stephenie does at times feel a bit awkward about these sorts of honours and awards but she would soon get more used to them. She would have to – because she was being honoured and recognised by all manner of people, societies, publications and companies. The giant Web company MSN, for instance, named her as one of 2008's most influential women.

'The former English major and Brigham Young grad claims that she never sought a career in writing,' read the announcement. 'In fact, she was perfectly content being a full-time mother to three boys. But after penning *Twilight*, a book based on a relationship between a male vampire and a high-school student, she was transformed into a literary luminary with a book debuting at number five on the *New York Times* bestseller list. Her fame rose in 2008 once *Twilight* was adapted for the big screen. The casting of English actor Robert Pattinson as Edward Cullen, the male vampire, sent female fans into hysterics and sold out theatres everywhere. The movie earned $72 million during [its] opening weekend, giving Meyers [*sic*] a blood-sucking success any author would want to sink her teeth into.'

The *Arizona Republic* joined in the worship, honouring her as one of its 'most fascinating people' of the moment. In announcing this award, it summed up well just how Stephenie's stock had risen and how she had slightly mixed feelings. 'It has been a big year for Meyer, who also released her first piece of adult fiction, *The Host*, an alien love story set near Picacho Peak, north of Tucson [Arizona]. The book promptly hit the best-seller list and stayed there. She appeared in *People* and *USA Today*, *Entertainment Weekly* devoted its cover to the *Twilight* tale. Her book tour for *Breaking Dawn*, the fourth *Twilight* volume, was a ticketed event and sold out across the country. She's starting to get recognized at the grocery store and at Target, much to her chagrin.'

Just as Stephenie became hugely famous as a result of her books, so too did the areas they were set in – most notably the little town of Forks, setting for much of the *Twilight* saga. The effect on the people of Forks has been incredible, and the local economy is now dominated by *Twilight*-related ventures, both official and unofficial. Annette and Tim Root plan to open the first *Twilight*-themed restaurant in the Forks area. They are due to name it Volterra, after the Italian city that features in the *Twilight* series.

Annette Root, the *Twilight*-themed restaurant owner, was not a natural for the vampire novel. A social worker living in Vancouver, she was told about the series by a friend and was far from convinced that the books were right for her. 'I rolled my eyes – teens, romance, vampires, yeah, right,' she said. However, once she started reading *Twilight* she was quickly hooked and soared through the series. With her obsession growing, eventually she, her husband and their children moved to Forks. 'He loved it even more than me because he is a small-town boy,' she said.

The Roots also own a *Twilight* shop, which stocks official, licensed products but also some made by fans. 'We have a lot of consignment,' Annette said. 'That is because my heart really is with the fan-created projects.' Annette Root also runs *Twilight* tours around the area. These include the early-morning *Breaking Dawn* tour, the three-hour Volturi tour and others.

There is already a bar called the Twilight Lounge in the area, at which an act called the Mitch Hansen Band have performed showing their *Twilight*-themed repertoire. There is also a Dew Drop Hotel (which includes a Bella Suite in honour of the *Twilight* heroine, with black curtains and crimson tulle wall swags, chocolates and sparkling cider served in champagne glasses) and a restaurant called Sully's Burgers, which has a pineapple-topped dish known as the Bella Burger. It is served complete with plastic fangs.

Then there are bowls and cups of Cullen Clam Chowder to be bought and Twilight Brew espressos. Shops stock numerous *Twilight* merchandise and unofficially themed products, which the visiting fans love to spend their money on. These include *Twilight* T-shirts sold at Jerry's Lock & Key and the 'Vampires Suck' shot glasses sold at a nearby store.

Another local store owner recounts how the *Twilight* sensation effectively saved her business. A long-standing flowers-and-gift shop run by Charlene Leppell was struggling but in the wake of the explosion of *Twilight* popularity she printed 'Bella for Prom Queen' T-shirts and added apples coated in shiny red ceramic to the shop's products. The sales were so plentiful that she renamed the store Twilight Central and upped the vampire theme. Soon her business was completely turned round. 'The question isn't whether I could afford to take a vacation this year,' Leppell said, 'but whether I could take off time from the store.'

Randy Lato runs a boat trip called 'Vampire Voyage,' even though he admits, 'I've only read two books in my entire life, and *Twilight* was not one of them.'

Even before the multitudes of fans arrive in the town proper, they will notice signposts to their destination. On the highway that leads to Forks there is a sandwich board sign saying 'Fangs whitened here' and just outside the town is a sign that reads 'Now entering Twilight Zone'. Such is the admiration and excitement of the visitors to Forks that the city officials had to move the 'City of Forks welcomes you' sign that stands on the border of the city, for fear of a serious traffic accident. Visiting *Twilight* fans would screech to a halt in their cars when they saw the sign, prompting fears that there would be a pile-up of cars one day. To minimise the probability of such a tragedy, the city officials moved the sign to a steep hill. 'Someone was going to get hurt,' Mayor Nedra Reed said. 'I was having nightmares about getting sued.'

There are mixed feelings among some locals about the overnight fame that Stephenie's stories have brought to their city. 'You can't drive through town sometimes easily because there are fans taking photographs all along the way and they slow the traffic down,' one said. 'It's a pretty minor price to pay.'

Other ambivalent comments have been forthcoming from locals. 'I do think it's a wonderful thing for our town, but it's definitely changed it, to say the least,' said one. 'So many people are upset.'

Another Forks resident was simply confused. 'I don't really understand why people come up to Forks because of a fictional book,' he said.

The switch from anonymity to becoming the focus of obsessive attention from *Twilight* fans has been a strange experience for the residents of the quiet area, which has a population of 3,120 (based on the 2000 census). 'You used to say you were from Forks and people would stare,' said Marcia Bingham, director of the Chamber of Commerce, referring to what she calls the 'BT' days (before *Twilight*). 'Now, when they hear where you're from, they're breathless.'

Outside the visitor centre stands 'Bella's truck' and those who step inside the centre can wear a white lab coat that has 'Dr Cullen' printed on it (a reference to Carlisle Cullen, head of the Cullen family, who works as a doctor at the local hospital, having long mastered control over the arousing effect that the sight and odour of human blood has on many of his kind).

Nearby in Port Angeles, an area also often mentioned in the *Twilight* books, the effect has been profound too. The local Bella Italia restaurant is the venue where Bella and Edward have their first ever date in the book. During that date, Bella orders a plate of mushroom ravioli. The result on the store can be seen by the fact that in 2009 the owner estimates that sales of the dish spectacularly soared to the region of 5,000 dishes.

A nearby newsagent, which Bella mentions in the novel, says that trade increased by 20 per cent in the wake of the book's publication. This is remarkable enough in itself, but all the more so when you consider that Bella does not even enter the store in the story but merely mentions it in passing, saying, 'It wasn't what I was looking for.' Even a passing, negative remark from Bella is enough to send thousands of fans to an otherwise unremarkable store. A local park that features in the story saw visitor numbers increase by 7 per cent after *Twilight* hit the bestseller lists. The Pacific Inn Motel has opened a *Twilight*-themed guestroom, with red and black guestrooms, posters from the cinema versions of the film and *Twilight* towels, which have drawn admiring comments from visiting fans.

Similarly, the Kalaloch Lodge may be 35 miles outside Forks but it still joins in the cash-in. The hotel offers a *New Moon–Twilight* package that includes a night in a log cabin, dessert and *Twilight* water bottle, from $149 per night.

In honour of Stephenie, Forks now celebrates an annual Stephenie Meyer Day on 13 September, the date of Bella Swan's birthday. No wonder there is such excitement in the area, with all this activity and profit coming from Stephenie's pen. 'It's a huge boon. We couldn't get publicity like this ever, paying for it,' said Marcia Bingham, at the Forks Chamber of Commerce.

It's not just fans who journey to Forks in hope of a bit of *Twilight* spirit. One of the regular visitors to the city is Stephenie herself. 'We have a little house we love to rent,' she enthuses. 'There's bald eagles' nests in the backyard. For us, that's a big deal.'

Fame for Stephenie has been a strange thing for her to cope with. She is not an attention grabber by nature, after all. 'I don't know, really. I used to live without being recognised. When I'm stopped on the road, I'm always shocked. People are always very kind. Some mothers come and see me, telling me that they have read *Twilight* with their daughters. That they are closer now. I think it's exciting to provoke this kind of situation.'

Her stature grows all the time, soaring higher and higher. In the closing months of 2009, the influential, respected *Vanity Fair* magazine named a list of important people whom it dubbed members of 'The New Establishment'. At number 82 in their list of 100 such people was Stephenie. 'The Mormon housewife's *Twilight* teen-vampire romance novels sold nearly 29 million copies in one year, capturing the top four positions on the *USA Today* best-seller list for 2008, making her the first author ever to do so,' read the explanatory text. 'The movie version of *Twilight* grossed $191 million in the US, and the film adaptation of her second book, *New Moon*, opens in November [2009]. Meyer has also inspired hundreds of Web sites from fans who call themselves "Stephenites" or "Twihards."'

At the end of the piece of text concerning each person on the list was a prediction for the year ahead. An arrow would point up, sideways or down, to signify an improvement, no change or a decrease in the person's stature in the year to come. The journal predicted that Stephenie would be on the up.

Even Oxford University has joined in the love-fest for Stephenie's novels. In October 2009, the prestigious British establishment published a list of typical questions asked at interview of prospective English students. One was 'Why might it be useful for an English student to read the *Twilight* series?' To have questions asked about her books, alongside questions covering Shakespeare and others, was yet another feather in Stephenie's literary cap.

There was controversy amid all this worship. In August 2009, a 'cease and desist' order was sent to her publisher by lawyers acting for Jordan Scott. The note claimed that *Breaking Dawn* 'shows a striking and substantial similarity' to Scott's book *The Nocturne*, and asks the publisher how it intends 'to cease and desist from any further copyright infringement and to compensate my client for her damages'. The mother company of Stephenie's publishers, Hachette, called the claim 'completely without merit'. It insisted that neither Stephenie nor her agent 'had any knowledge of this writer or her supposed book prior to this claim. Ms Scott's attorney has yet to furnish us with a copy of the book to support this claim as requested,' the statement said. 'The world of *The Twilight Saga* and the stories within it are entirely the creation of Ms Meyer. Her books have been a phenomenal sensation, and perhaps it shouldn't be surprising to hear that other people may seek to ride the coattails of such success. This claim is frivolous and any lawsuit will be defended vigorously.'

This had echoes of the experience of J K Rowling. In 2001, she received a claim from author Nancy Stouffer that the *Harry Potter* series featured ideas from books she had written during the 1980s: one featured a character called Larry Potter; another featured 'muggles' (muggles in the world of Potter are ordinary, non-magical folk; in Stouffer's novel they're mutant humanoids). The court found in favour of Rowling, and all in Stephenie's camp remain optimistic and insistent that the Scott case will be found in their heroine's favour.

Meanwhile, Stephenie was full of excitement as the movie world prepared for the launch of the *New Moon* film. Here she would see another of her books adapted for the big screen. She was as excited ahead of the November 2009 launch as any of her fans. 'Can't November come any quicker?' she wrote on her website, adding, 'When it comes to *New Moon*, you haven't seen anything yet!'

Two months before it hit the screens, the early showings of the film had sold out in many cinemas. 'For many fans, it's clearly the year's most anticipated film event,' said the ticketing service Fandango's chief operating officer, Rick Butler. 'Ever since tickets went on sale on August 31, it's been among our top five weekly ticket-sellers. We're seeing a higher-than-usual number of tickets per transaction for this film, suggesting that moviegoers will show up en masse at theaters this weekend with their friends and family.'

What sort of film would they see? During the production – followed closely as ever by the Twihards – many rumours had flown around. There had been talk that Taylor Lautner would be replaced in the part of Jacob, but happily he got the nod to continue. 'I was very much a part of this decision,' said Stephenie. 'My first priority was always what was best for *New Moon* – what was going to give us the best possible movie. I'm truly thrilled that Taylor was the one who proved to the director, to Summit and to me that he is the best possible Jacob we could have. And I'm very much looking forward to seeing what he's going to bring to Jacob's character this year.'

However, *Twilight*'s director Catherine Hardwicke did fly the nest, to Stephenie's dismay. 'I'm sad that Catherine is not continuing on with us for *New Moon*. I'm going to miss her, not just as a brilliant director, but also as a friend. She has such a distinct, authentic voice that did amazing things for *Twilight*. I'm looking forward to every movie she does in the future.'

Hardwicke was replaced by Chris Weitz, who had directed *American Pie*, *About a Boy* and *The Golden Compass*. In a typical Hollywood moment, he announced his gratitude for Stephenie's 'permission to protect *New Moon* in its translation from the page to the screen'. He also spoke of his 'whirlwind romance' with the books.

Stephenie has said that she expected *New Moon* to be a difficult book to transfer to film, 'but lucky for us Chris Weitz is a genius!'

The week before the film's launch, Stephenie gave an interview to *The Oprah Winfrey Show*. She had been relatively shy of media attention for a while before this, so there was a lot of interest in what she would have to say. *Twilight* fans sat on the edges of their seats as Winfrey – going into a commercial break – said, 'Coming up, will there be a fifth book in the *Twilight* saga? Stephenie answers that later.' However, the question was never answered on the show, because Winfrey didn't get the chat round to that topic.

Mindful that having trailed such a killer question they had a responsibility to follow up, some of Oprah's staff approached Stephenie behind the scenes and asked that very question. 'I can't answer it. The way I write, it's what makes me happy. Like, I can't write when people are looking over my shoulder,' she replied.

She admitted that she was somewhat tired of the genre. 'I am a little burned out on vampires right now,' she said. 'I think I need a little break. I might go spend some time with my aliens. I might do something completely different. I've got to cleanse the palate. I may come back to it. I did envision it as a longer series. But I wrapped at *Breaking Dawn* in a way that I felt satisfied with, so, if that moment didn't come, I'd be OK.'

But did she, asked the researcher, have an idea what would happen to Edward and Bella in the future? 'Oh, absolutely,' said Stephenie confidently. 'I know exactly what happens.' The researcher speculated that Stephenie wouldn't say. Absolutely not, of course. 'Sorry,' giggled Stephenie.

She confirmed that *The Host* was due a return. 'It's kind of my favourite thing I've ever done. I see that as a three-book series, so I'll probably get back into that one again. We're working on the movie at the moment so I'm spending time with the characters, so that's something I might go back to again.'

She also announced she was working on a fantasy

novel. 'So fantasy that there's a map in the front – if there's a map, that's real fantasy.'

With the making of the movie *Eclipse* just completed, she was able to give a hint of what viewers can expect when that is released later in 2010. 'The action keeps getting better. With *Twilight* it was a lot more boy and girl; we didn't get a ton of action. In *New Moon*, of course, there's a whole bunch more – the CGI [computer-generated imagery] literally takes your breath away. In the next one we have a lot more vampire action and the vampires are going to be able to run real fast. It's cool. I think it's my favourite effect so far.'

Asked how it felt to meet the actors who played her literary characters, she described the experience as 'crazy, surreal'.

Crazy was just the word for the excitement, the hysteria, one could almost say, that greeted the release of the *New Moon* movie in November 2009. Ahead of the premiere, hundreds of *Twilight* fans camped out outside Mann's Village Theatre in Westwood, Los Angeles. They hoped to catch a glimpse of the arriving cast, crew and – of course – Stephenie.

As with the launches of her novels, there were themed parties and events to help fans get in the mood. These included the New Moon Experience, a two-day bash arranged by the aforementioned *Twilight Moms* website. Ahead of the premiere, the cast spoke of the effect that the fame they gained from their involvement in Stephenie's stories had on their families.

'My family is embarrassingly proud of me,' said Kristen Stewart (Bella). 'My brothers get a little protective. I've made rules now that you can't go outside and scream at people with cameras.'

Robert Pattinson (Edward) said, 'My family live in London and I think they don't really realise what's been going on in America.'

The early reviews for *New Moon* were promising, with praise also forthcoming for the film's soundtrack, a development that will have pleased music-mad Stephenie. That said, the praise from *Total Film* magazine was rather a mixed experience for her. 'Seriously, this will get people into cinemas who had no interest whatsoever in Stephenie Meyer's vampire frolics/bollocks,' it read.

New Moon was guaranteed to be a huge hit in the cinema, just as *Twilight* was. These successes are the source of gigantic pride to Stephenie. Meanwhile, she continues to write. Since the day that she wrote the first passage of what became *Twilight*, in the wake of that tremendous dream, her writing process has changed in some ways.

'It has,' she confirmed. 'It's gone through some evolutions as I experiment with different ways to do things. With *Twilight*, I didn't know it was going to happen when I wrote it. It just was writing to find out the answer. With the others I had to start outlining. I had to be more careful because I knew when I started the sequel, *New Moon*, where it was going to end, so that takes a lot more work to tie up the threads. And I've experimented with a couple of other things on the side, so I haven't really consolidated what I do. The biggest change is that when I started writing I had three kids under the school age all day. All my kids are in school full-time now so that really has been the biggest change in my writing style.'

While she says the *Twilight* series ends with the publication of *Breaking Dawn*, she knows that some fans are craving further instalments. While none should hold their breath for further sequels, they should not entirely give up hope either. 'It's done for now,' she says. 'I mean I can't promise that I won't get lonely for the Cullens and come back to them in ten years, but right now I feel really satisfied with where it is, so I'm not planning on doing anything with it – but, you know, no guarantees.'

Some of her fans have expressed a desire that the story remain closed. However, many more would dearly love to have another instalment of the *Twilight* series delivered into their hands. Given Stephenie's connection with and, indeed, love of her characters, will she be able to resist getting them out again and giving them another spin? After all, as we have seen, she has their futures plotted out in her mind already. It would take the sort of restraint that Edward showed with Bella for Stephenie to resist that path one day.

For now, though, she is content – to say the least – to

let the story rest. She recalls vividly her feeling when she realised that her work on the *Twilight* story was over. 'You know, it was funny because I was expecting this sense of closure when I finished the rough draft,' she said. 'I was expecting it again when I finished my editing and I knew it was going to print. But it wasn't until the books were out on the shelves that it was done and I had that sense of crossing the finish line, like, "I've done it! I've gotten it all done!"'

Although her novels have all been signed for big-screen adaptations, she is not about to 'cut out the middle man' and write a screenplay herself. 'I don't think I could,' she admits, 'unless Hollywood is ready for a fourteen-hour movie experience. I just don't think in short terms. I have to explore every tiny, little detail. I really admire people who can come in, streamline it and get all the information across so simply, but I can't imagine doing that – it's not my talent.'

Not that she is about to stop writing novels. There's a lot in the pipeline for Stephenie. 'I may write some sequels for *The Host*, or I may pull another outline from my files to play with,' she says. The options are plentiful, and a *Host* sequel seems likely, given that Stephenie has said, 'Those characters are really hard to put away.' She adds, 'I won't stop writing: there are too many stories I want to tell.'

There is even one book she has begun to write but put on the backburner – it is of a slightly surprising genre. 'The story was really sound, it was probably pretty good, except it was a chick-lit story,' she says. 'It was going to get funny, but I just got really bored with it. It was all humans, and that doesn't seem to be enough for me. I need a little element of fantasy to make it worth my interest.'

She may have put it to one side, but that does not mean she has completely abandoned it. 'It's stuck in the computer,' she says. 'Nothing's ever thrown away.'

She has also spoken of completing a ghost story called *Summer House* – 'I'm pretty excited about it because I get to make up my own world there' – and, as she had previously hinted, even possibly a novel involving mermaids: 'I love the idea, and I love the characters, but I don't know if I can do it.' She has also written a 'monster manual' for the fourth edition of the Dungeons & Dragons role-play game. It will be titled *Stephenie's Sanctum*.

The *Twilight* fanbase – or Twihards – give the impression to some observers of being an army. Their passion for the books, married to their ability on the Web, combined with the fact that, as teenage girls, the majority of them have plenty of leisure time, means that their force is felt keenly. However, Stephenie regards them more as family than army. 'I have all these teenage adopted daughters,' says the woman who has mothered only sons. 'They're impossible not to adore.' As in real families, there are people of both genders and all ages included. As Stephenie noted with admiration of the conduct of her fans at public events,

'It's the fifty-year-old women who are screaming the loudest!' Long may the family grow and prosper, with Stephenie at its head.

She has experienced enormous success very suddenly, thanks to the popularity of her books and the movies they spawned. 'I am continually shocked by the success of my books,' she says. Given that she began work on them by simply noting down the details of a dream, and that she continued to write them with only herself in mind as the reader – and then only ever imagined that she would see a handful of the books on sale at one small bookshop – she must indeed feel shocked by how well they have done.

The success has not changed her, though. 'I never take it for granted, and I do not count on it in my expectations in the future. It's a very enjoyable thing, and I'll have fun with it while it lasts. I've always considered myself first and foremost a mother, so being a writer hasn't changed my life too much – except that I do travel a lot more and have less free time.'

She remains in her own mind a mother before anything else, then a wife, daughter and sibling, and then an author. That said, she feels her books – and the characters therein – are great creations that have helped bring a little bit extra to her family. 'I love my kids. Each one of them is worth everything, and all three of them are worth everything times three, but I needed something extra, my way to be me,' Meyer says. 'I did feel like something was missing. There was a lot of creativity that wasn't making it out. That's probably why it came out in such a gush. It was a relief to have something that was just me. It's hard when you don't have any conversation outside of "Mommy, poo-poo,"' she says. 'Imaginary characters work well. I think I've always been a storyteller. I was just too shy to ever tell them.'

Just as she is a proud parent, so are her parents proud of her, if a little surprised by the enormous success of her writing career. 'We wouldn't have guessed that she was going to have this kind of experience in her life,' says Stephen Morgan, her father, who, along with Stephenie's mother Candy and elder sister Emily, reads everything she writes before she submits it to any professional eye. 'I'm proud of her for the kind of mother she is. And I'm proud that she's staying true to who she is, even though, when there's a thousand people cheering for you, it's not easy. I'm happy for her that that's the way she is.'

And 'the way she is' is entirely modest and unchanged by her success. She is regularly seen at her local eatery, the Horny Toad restaurant. 'Stephenie and the boys come in here for burgers but she doesn't expect any special treatment,' said a waitress. 'We just treat her the same as everyone else. She was Stephenie long before all this craziness started. She's not one to ever make a fuss. The only difference these days is she orders salad with her burger instead of fries. She's trying to watch her figure. She says the press pictures always make her look fat.'

She lives in Cave Creek, Arizona. Her home is nice, but rather modest for a woman of her wealth. It is a four-bedroom house set at the end of a trail. It blends into the surrounding desert quietly enough with its sand-coloured exterior. However, the house is surrounded by metal gates and has a security video camera monitoring passers-by, many of whom are *Twilight* fans. Neighbours give short shrift to any visiting reporters or fans who try to dig some dirt on the author. 'Around here people value their privacy and keep themselves to themselves,' says one unnamed, cowboy-boot-wearing neighbour. 'The desert is where you come to get away from the world. Out here the only stars are in the sky.'

For the fans, though, Stephenie is the biggest star in the literary firmament. Just as many fans hang on to her fictional words, so do they value her real-life thoughts. One of the legacies that she has already left on the world – and how wonderfully strange to speak of legacies left by a healthy woman still in her thirties – is that she has injected yet more literary passion into a generation that some thought had left the joys of reading long behind, all the better to concentrate on their iPods, satellite television boxes and websites. Not only has she got them flocking in their millions into bookshops around the world, she has also created a new army of budding authors. For most of these would-be Stephenie Meyers, dreams will remain just that. However, for some the dream could come true and they too could taste the wonders of literary fame just as she did.

So how, many of her fans cannot help but wonder, does Stephenie do it? How do you take authorial aspirations and turn them into something real and living on the printed page, something that people will rush to their local bookshop to get their hands on? Not all can hope for the outrageous fortune of being struck one night by a vivid dream that would turn into a publishing and cinematic sensation. Indeed, not even Stephenie herself imagines that she will be so lucky again. Not that she believes she needs to be in order to carry on writing.

'You don't get a dream like that twice,' she says. 'I got my chance and I feel like I was supposed to be writing, and this dream was my kick in the pants to get going. Once I'd started it, I didn't need another dream because, once I discovered how wonderful writing was for me, I was ready to go with it.' Even the scale of your education need not matter, she tells people. 'You don't need any degree at all to be published,' she says. 'Studying literature and the English language definitely does help with the writing. I learned everything I know about writing from all the reading I did in my life.'

For her, the characters have always been the most important part of her books. How should a would-be author go about trying to create her own imaginary figures, who could live, breathe and appeal like Edward, Bella and Jacob? In terms of character

234

development, she advised, 'I guess all I can say is, try to believe in your characters, let them live, and try to listen to them. Let them shape your stories around their true character, rather than trying to shove their character unnaturally into your story.'

So how – in a nutshell – should those Twihards or *Host* fans fulfil their dream and make it on to the published page as the next Stephenie Meyer? For her, the answer is dazzlingly simple: 'Believe that you can do it.' However, together with that belief, she says, it is vital to do one other thing – just get on with it. 'Treat it like a job,' she advises would-be authors. 'Write something every day. So many people have come up to me and said that they want to write a book, and I always laugh and say, "Well, why don't you do it?"'

It worked for her, though she remains as modest as ever. 'I don't think I'm a writer: I think I'm a storyteller,' she said. 'The words aren't always perfect.'

stephenie meyer bibliography

Series

Twilight, Little, Brown, 5 October 2005.
New Moon, Little, Brown, 6 September 2006.
Eclipse, Little, Brown, 7 August 2007.
Breaking Dawn, Little, Brown, 2 August 2008.

Novels

The Host, Little, Brown, 6 May 2008.

Collections

Prom Nights from Hell, HarperTeen, 24 April 2007.

bibliography

Albert, Lisa Rondinelli, *Stephenie Meyer: Author of the Twilight Saga*, Enslow Publishers, 2009.

Beahm, George, *Bedazzled: A Book About Stephenie Meyer and the Twilight Phenomenon*, Underwood Books, 2009.

Housel, Rebecca and J Jeremy Wisnewski, *Twilight and Philosophy: Vampires, Vegetarians and the Pursuit of Immortality*, Wiley, 2009.

Howden, Martin, *Blood Rivals*, John Blake, 2009.

Twenge, Jean M, *Generation Me: Why Today's Young Americans Are More Confident, Assertive, Entitled – And More Miserable Than Ever Before*, Free Press, 2007.